THE EXPERIMENT

THE EXPERIMENT

AN EXPLORATION OF PERCEPTION AND FOCUS

A PRIMER

BY

KETHERIN MICHAELS AND CORVUS NIGHT

GREYBEAR PUBLISHING CO.
SANTA FE, NEW MEXICO

GREYBEAR PUBLISHING CO.
PO BOX 5158
SANTA FE, NEW MEXICO 87502

<u>Note to the reader</u> ie. the small print

This book contains exercises in meditation and breathing intended to expand the awareness into levels that are normally invisible to the waking consciousness. The reader is responsible for maintaining a balanced control over any meditations or exercises attempted. The authors and publishers take no responsibility for any results that might occur from the performance of these meditations or exercises. If you do not agree to accept these guidelines, you may return the book for a full refund.

Printed in Canada by Friesens, Inc.

Edited by Kate Correa

LCCN: 2001096339

Publisher's Cataloging-in-Publication Data

Michaels, Ketherin.
    The experiment, an exploration of perception and focus. A primer / by Ketherin Michaels and Corvus Night. -- 1st ed.
        p. cm.
        Includes bibliographical references
        ISBN 0-9703103-5-8

    1. New Age movement. 2. Metaphysics I. Night, Corvus. II. Title.

BP605.N48M53 2002   299'.93
                QB101-701094

ACKNOWLEDGEMENTS

This book is dedicated to
our very dear and
supportive friends for
their love, patience and
constant encouragement,
for without them
there would be no book.

Our special thanks to
The Hawk,
living proof that
"where there's a Will,
there's a way!"

TABLE OF CONTENTS

THE ILLUSTRATIONS

PUBLISHER'S NOTE

Above the entrance to Apollo's temple at Delphi was inscribed the following statement,

"KNOW THYSELF"

To know one's true self is to know the cosmos and all that is within it. Easier said than done. And yet every seeker after truth is challenged by these words which echo through the centuries, calling us home, so to speak. For to know thyself is a different sort of knowledge than to know science or mathematics, or literature. To know thyself is to turn within to seek and find that which exists at the core of one's being. Living in a culture that emphasizes the outward show makes the search perhaps more difficult but at the same time more urgent.

Maps and guideposts abound, from the Tao of Lao Tzu, to the philosophers of ancient Greece, from the shamanic wisdom of Australia to present day occult psychology and magic. This book that you hold is a map, a guide, a teacher and a friend. It has been around for twenty years in manuscript form and has helped and inspired many. Now, in the new millennium, it is time for it to reach a wider audience, and we have been charged to make it so.

THE EXPERIMENT is one that we are asked to perform on ourselves. It is the nature of an experimenter to try something out and then observe the results. This leads to further experimentation and observation. As THE EXPERIMENT continues, we discover, or uncover layers of truth about how we perceive reality and how we use the power of focus to create our life experience.

This first book of THE EXPERIMENT, A PRIMER, is an introduction, an overview. It wastes no time plunging the reader into the thick of new concepts, new terms, new ways of looking at the world. If you find yourself reading something you don't understand, relax. Look at the pictures, read it over, or just go on. In time, all becomes clear and you find yourself in a world of beauty, love and excitement - the excitement of being an explorer,

an inner space traveler.

Good luck on the journey.

J. Grey & Jade Easton
GreyBear Publishing Co
Santa Fe   2001

FOREWORD

The Experiment is a truly stunning work of art and knowledge in the design and color, ideas and consciousnesses it contains. What great challenges it offers in enlarging upon our ordinary practices of living in our everyday realities! This book is so fascinating, so creative and colorful and penetrating, that it can be studied many times as we seek to enhance our ordinary, habitual understanding of who and what we really are, and can be, on so many intimate levels of consciousness.

Just like its text, color, blessed color, rings throughout The Experiment in unique ways, helping us grasp its deeply creative meaning. I've never seen color used so beautifully, containing within it the essence of all we have been, are, and will be. Yet both color and text help us explore the treasures of our psyches in new ways, opening up their mysteries so that consciously we can dip into, explore, our own wonders. My reality will never be the same - how fine it is that The Experiment can help us embark upon our new creative journeys. How fine to learn and know more - much more - about who and what we are so that we can communicate better not only with ourselves but with others. What a pleasure to behold the new realities The Experiment opens up as we study it.

Robert F. Butts

PREFACE

In 1976, I closed the door on an old life, and stepped into the unknown. Because of the unusual circumstances in which I found myself, the new life presented me with an opportunity, perhaps even the necessity, to do something I had always dreamt of doing. I began studying with a teacher who instructed me in learning to still the chatter of the *small me* voice, to experience the Inner Silence. The energy that moves us to look into ourselves and find answers, call it curiosity or passion, drove me, or rather pulled me into a serious attempt to communicate with Larger Teachers on a broader, wider plane to explore the philosophy of life.

From 1976 through 1980 I studied and practiced. In a regular routine, I would, with increasing success, silence the *small me* chatter and write down everything I heard. I was finally able to fine tune my focus so as to consistently hear the Voice of A Teacher.

Suffice it to say that I went through tedious fits of insecurity and nagging self doubts, until, by repeated tests, I came to a secure and proven belief in what I was hearing. Through repetition my confidence grew and I began to accept the reality of the instructions from the Inner Planes.

THE EXPERIMENT is the account of my philosophical journey on the Inner Planes, to a dimension of pure thought and idea that the teachers describe as *THE CONCEPT POOL*.

On the outer planes, teachers everywhere instruct the seekers. I primarily rested on a solid base of four teachers, each a complement to the others; for me, an unbeatable combination. Don Juan and his exalted lineage of Toltec Men and Women of Knowledge, brought to us by don Carlos Castaneda, showed me the necessity of living an impeccable life. The Master, Paul Foster Case, walked with me, step by step, and taught me how to achieve silence so I could hear the Inner teachings. Seth, brought to us by the team of Jane Roberts and Robert Butts, ignited my sense of adventure and opened my mind to the possibilities of what was to be discovered. And last, but never least, the consistent guidelines and good advice of the Wilhelm/Baynes translation of the I Ching dispensed great wisdom through all the aspects of my life.

The teachings of so many tell us that the Universe is MENTAL, THE ALL IS MIND. On any inner quest we are led into the Mind, our own Mind . . . and, lo and behold, we find that there are many courses of training, WITHIN, that teach the seeker how to explore this new realm and use this tool, our own mind, to reach The Larger Mind.

The assumption I ask the reader to share is that we are far more than the small specific earth 'me' - that there is an Inner Reality - a larger order and harmony to life than the earth appearance seems to imply.

The word "awareness," whose root meaning is "together," or "complete," best describes our human function, our link to the Cosmic Mind, the Life Force. *Awareness, consciousness, perception, focus* - these are some of the terms that identify the areas of exploration and training in THE EXPERIMENT.

Unfortunately, this Inner Journey is often considered dangerous. The western society that values the mental faculty of reason, paradoxically, distrusts other less developed qualities of the mind. Organized religion, medicine and even science, that great definer of the Twentieth Century, warn of the dangers of turning within to search the Inner Realms. Yet there are many teachers who instruct us in getting to these Inner Realms safely, to begin to find answers to that age-old question, "What Is Life All About?"

The teachings I received from the Concept Pool are a semi-scientific, somewhat metaphysical view. They describe life, as experienced through our perception on earth, as An Experiment in Consciousness. They challenge us to remember where we extend beyond our earth selves, for THE EXPERIMENT is a journey into Our Own Selves, into our extensions - the part of us that the every-day world would often have us forget or deny.

As the teachers constantly stressed, entering new realms of thought is an athletic endeavor, mentally athletic. The challenge is to achieve the mental flu-idity to stretch the mind's capacity beyond everyday considerations, even when the new ideas seem outlandish, or improbable. One of the basic stretches comes with the concept of *mirror living*, the idea that we see and experience life reversed, similar to a view in a mirror. This is a basic premise of THE EXPERIMENT, and one that took a bit of getting used to, but as I came to accept the reality, the proof of the new Laws I was learning, my whole definition structure shifted, and I finally began to achieve the fluidity the teachers demanded of me.

I was instructed to look in between things, into what I had defined as hid-den or invisible, never to stop short at the limits of the old definitions. No idea or concept was allowed to remain static. There were always possibilities to be considered, variations to be taken into account, and on top of that I probably had to reverse whatever it was I was considering and see it from other angles.

When the teachers refer to the third eye, and how we are to use this elu-sive ability, they speak as though it were a simple enough achievement. It was in the constant shifting of definitions that somehow my awareness, my focus achieved new expanded dimensions. I could see more than ever before, under-stand and experience with greater depth and awareness. This, they informed me, was evidence that the third eye was beginning to open. They told me con-stantly that keeping an open and fluid mind was an athletic achievement and that I should approach it as such.

I did. And one June morning, in 1980, my Teacher on the Inner Planes prepared and reassured me. I then experienced a dramatic switch, to another channel, a higher level. I entered an Immensity, a Grand Cavernous Vastness, where Larger Beings, in deep, resonating voices embraced me in their Love, and spoke to me. With this Initial Contact, the first book of THE EXPERIMENT began.

THE EXPERIMENT was written in about three years, with sessions held three times a week, and everything recorded. The Primer covers material heard in the first six weeks of sessions. It is a series of *turnarounds* that the student is taken through in preparation for the volumes in THE EXPERIMENT that follow.

At the same time, in sessions that were separate, my partner, Corvus Night, and I were being instructed in number and music theory, and we began making charts of the musical keys and designs built on the number seven. Since THE EXPERIMENT begins with these very charts, Corvus, whose encouragement gave me confidence, and whose understanding and illustrations of the information lends order and coherence to the books, will help prepare you in A Point Of View for the often mind-stretching experience of reading what these Larger Entities from the Inner Planes would like to share with us.

If learning to see the world as these teachers do is even half the fun it was for us, then I know we can join together on this Inner Journey, hopefully into a better, more aligned new century.

We pass this information on, assured that some will welcome it with open arms, others will scoff, some will doubt. Yet pass it on we do, for that too is part of the instructions, to let these books move through reality, blending with the other Rivers of New Thought that prepare us all for a New Age.

K. Michaels

A POINT OF VIEW

HIDDEN DIMENSIONS

Things are seldom what they appear to be. Appearances are linked to perception and perception is relative. What you see depends upon your viewpoint and there are as many points of view as there are pairs of eyes to see.

Throughout the ages, religious aspirants, philosophers and scientists have searched for a deeper understanding of life in order to extend the powers and the limits of being human, of living on earth. Very often the searcher after truth is guided into dimensions where information is available from sources that seem to exist beyond the three-dimensional framework we call earth existence.

THE EXPERIMENT originates from such a hidden dimension, and it invites us to consider the existence of a multifaceted structure of realities, the one we call three-dimensional earth being only one aspect in an infinite array of possible existences. These realities co-exist with ours in time and space, and are accessible to the traveller who can extend the imagination to accept the idea of invisible worlds.

The concept of infinitely layered realities has been known and taught for countless thousands of years. In other, less hidebound ages, aspects of these ideas were widely accepted and practiced. Even in this age, many cultures would find the image of a multidimensional structure of worlds quite reasonable, as their description of reality includes invisible realms which are accessible through the use of the inward looking senses.

With the development of western society and culture in the last few thousand years, the knowledge and use of our inner senses has been progressively covered over, resulting in greater and greater dependence on the outer, bodily senses. The current situation could be described using the computer acronym, *WYSIWYG*, "What You See Is What You Get," or the inverse: if you don't see it, feel it, hear it, smell it or taste it, it probably doesn't exist.

In the cave analogy in Plato's <u>Republic</u>, Socrates explains how this bondage of the senses operates and illustrates how all layers of perception are relative, depending upon our viewpoint. On one layer the prisoners of the cave are shackled from childhood, forced throughout life to gaze straight ahead seeing only a wall covered with moving light and shadows.

The light is from a fire, unseen, behind the prisoners. The flickering patterns on the wall are the shadows from a procession of objects that are held and moved so that their shadows are cast upon the wall. The voices of the people carrying the various shapes back and forth echo off the wall and sound to the prisoners as if they come from the shadows.

In time, the prisoners have a tradition that encompasses all the known conditions of the wall. Generations of focus have made the wall the only conceivable reality. There develops a hierarchy of those with the keenest sight, those who can follow the flickering images more closely than others and describe what is happening, never suspecting that they all see only the grossest distortion of the "true reality."

If any of the prisoners had ever suspected that *reality* was behind them and around them, out of sight, that view had long since been overwhelmed by the evidence which was right before their eyes. If a prisoner were turned around to face the procession of objects and told that these were the reality and the shadows merely reflections, that person would have difficulty even seeing the objects, his eyes would be so blinded by the light from the fire. Only by degrees would he learn to adjust to the new view, the next layer of perception, and if the prisoner were taken from the cave into the world of sunlight, he would find this layer even more disturbing and difficult to perceive.

To Socrates, the prison house of the cave was an analogy for the way that the sense of vision limits the mind and the imagination by binding our attention to an outer reality of objects and appearances. He warned that the visible world we call real can overwhelm the less compelling stimuli that often come to us from invisible inner sources. The habitual emphasis on what we see leads us to an over-fixation on outward appearances, resulting in a life as narrowly confined as that of the prisoners of the cave.

To offset this tendency there are always people like Socrates among us; individuals who have penetrated the veil of the illusion and caught a glimpse of a clearer and more comprehensive view of life. These people open doors to the inner realms for the willing and adventurous to explore. Not all want to follow these paths. Few know they are there. Fewer still actually walk them.

As a result, the knowledge of our true state remains hidden, and most people hold a limited view of reality, accepting wars and suffering as inescapable, ignoring the fact that we live in a wonderful and inconceivably well-ordered universe.

Yet this knowledge is available to anyone seeking it, and now, as we approach a new age, many are impelled to find an alternative to the contradictions of modern existence. Many look to find a connection to something larger within themselves that is not affected by outer turmoil and which will provide stability and continuity in a time of increasing outer uncertainty.

We are on the threshold now, entering a new era when the inner paths of knowledge and truth will be more widely known and travelled. As we cross over, we can look back and see where we, in the western cultures, developed the collective *blind spot* which sidetracks or distracts us from pursuing inner knowledge.

MYTH? . . . HISTORY?

If we look back through recorded history, the accounts of life grow more and more sketchy. We are taught little about earlier civilizations beyond what archaeologists and historical anthropologists have "discovered." But if we look into stories that are thought of as Myth, we find some clues about when and how the masking of our inner senses took place.

Stories have come out of early Egypt which tell of a people under the guidance of the legendary Priest-Kings, rulers who maintained and fostered the link with Spirit and who taught their people to look within and find the harmony which is the basis of life on earth. It is said that through mental discipline these rulers exercised great powers. Their chariots were drawn by wild lions under their mental control. They built the pyramids, not with thousands of slaves, but by training the populace in working with sound to shape and move the giant blocks. In stories like this we glimpse back to a time before the blind spot developed.

In Walton's retelling of the Mabinogion, the Welsh mythic history (see Bibliography), the writer speaks of a coming veil or shroud of darkness that was to be drawn over the minds of men, so that they would forget their origins, forget the old magic. This coming darkness was linked with a time when the world would turn outward, away from a dependence on the nurturing power of the Great Mother, the female principle, and toward a reliance upon men and their deeds of domination, which often entailed war and acts of cruelty.

Turning to Hebrew myth and history in the Old Testament, we see a polarity developing. In the Eden myth, before the fall, humans knew of their oneness with Spirit (THE ALL). This enabled them to experience the Unity of life and to know its goodness. By "eating the apple," they cut themselves off from the natural state of union where ALL is good, and plunged into a state called "the knowledge of good *and* evil."

This transition represents not the entry into original sin (the Great Lie), but rather an entry into a level of consciousness where human personality would be tested in the fires of the *appearance of opposites*, to be forged and shaped into an instrument with finely tuned perceptions. When essential goodness appears on stage as the polarity of good and evil, the players are often confronted by turbulent appearances of suffering and lack, and confused by the interplay of opposites and contradiction. Success in this venture depends upon each individual seeing through the appearance of opposites to develop a link to the (hidden) underlying Unity that brings resolution to the world of opposites.

In Hebrew history, the Israelites succeeded only by allowing their actions to be guided by the Divine Spirit within them. The need to maintain a conscious link with the Inner Self, the Indivisible One, is a theme stressed throughout the Old Testament. The lives of the people who followed this path were blessed with abundance, wealth and fulfilment. Those who turned away from the inner guidance experienced suffering and lack.

The tradition of wisdom that guided the prophets of Israel keeps alive in all times the knowledge of humanity's true state, the knowledge that the Self dwells within, that the Garden of Eden is a state of mind, attainable here and now by learning to align with it - the concept of the kingdom of heaven within. This same wisdom is active through the Essenes and the Gnostic Christians, and later surfaces in the Tarot and the Rosicrucian Order.

The other pole of the Hebrew tradition is visible in the description of the Old Testament god, a righteous, vengeful, male, warrior god who demands unquestioning obedience and who alternately delivers the Israelites into the hands of their enemies or vice-versa, depending upon the peoples' behavior. This is the god that became the model for successive generations of male-dominated societies typified by the Jewish high priesthood, the Romans, the Roman Catholic Church, fundamentalist religions, and by groups like the Puritans, the

Mafia and the military industrial complex, all of whose creed is: "obey us or suffer."

The Greeks took a more humanistic approach. Greek life and thought was strongly influenced by the mystery religions that flourished in Asia Minor. This was (and is) a tradition which reveres the Mother principle. This tradition cultivated a belief in all the hierarchies of consciousness, of gods and heroes, of satyrs, nymphs and dryads, and these forms were often visible to those humans who could extend their consciousness to perceive these co-existing layers of reality.

The acceptance of the invisible (to us) layers of being reflects in the easy way that Greek thought travelled between inner and outer realities, and this balance of visible and invisible experience provided a solid philosophical base for the flowering of Greece in the Golden Age. Their achievements are legendary, and their shining example has inspired the world for twenty-five centuries, but this pinnacle was also a crossover point, for the forces of self-denial that had Socrates killed were on the move.

SWING OF THE PENDULUM

By the time of the Roman Empire, the consciousness of the link between visible and invisible worlds had been greatly diminished. The pendulum of history was swinging 180 degrees: from the Hebrews, whose greatest leaders placed their trust in a divine inner power, to the Romans, whose temporal leaders claimed divinity, thus eliminating the mechanism in society whereby political ambition could be tempered by inner truth and justice. In the government and institutions of Rome, Divine Law was made lackey to self-interest, a tradition which continues in the political and economic institutions of today.

As the Roman Empire deteriorated, the Roman Church was rising to power with a new form of control. In the early years of the church in Rome a group of elders met to counter what they considered a growing threat from the Gnostic interpretation of the Christ experience. The church elders represented the Apostolic Succession, a church hierarchy which claimed a direct, physical line to Jesus through the apostle Peter and all the primates of Rome, through the "laying on of hands."

The Gnostics were spiritually related to the Essenes whom many believe were the sages who instructed Jesus in his youth. They held that anyone could commune directly with the Divine Spirit through an intuitive link and thus receive inspiration, support and guidance directly from the Source, ALL THAT IS, without the intervention of the church and the priesthood.

The elders of the Church in Rome saw that unless they could control the interpretation of Jesus' teachings, their organization would be splintered into innumerable sects, each with its own interpretation and body of scriptures. It was during this early Christian period that certain texts were altered or excluded from the canon of accepted scriptures. Among these were Essene writings which supported the Gnostic view of emancipation through Self knowledge.

The consolidation that the church fathers achieved was an insidious bid for power, and one which would have drawn the admiration and respect of the

Roman despots. The new doctrine denied our innate link with Spirit, and stated that as humans we are born into a state of original sin with a dead soul, that the only salvation is through the intervention of the priesthood and the sacraments.

Once distortions like these became rooted in the mind of the populace the power of the church was guaranteed. For fifteen hundred years it was the dominant economic, political and social force on the European continent. While disclaiming political ambition, it manipulated governments to its own ends by the threat of withholding the possibility of redemption. Through the practice of requiring tithes, it amassed great wealth for itself and its supporters. When its base of power began to erode, the Church launched the Inquisition in an attempt to maintain control through fear and persecution. Among the many targets of this persecution were people who practiced the ancient nature religions. This included midwives, herbalists and those who celebrated the changing of the seasons. It was not until the Reformation movement of Martin Luther in the 1500's that the Church's unilateral power was seriously threatened.

Luther's challenge loosened the stranglehold that the Catholic Church had over the minds of the people, freeing them to think for themselves. The renaissance in knowledge, art, science and technology which accompanied these developments was in direct proportion to the way the Roman Church had suppressed the free flow of ideas. The Church had always maintained that its canon was divinely inspired and that there was no need to expand upon it. Inquisitiveness and original thought were frowned on, and for 1700 years, scientific inquiry, though it flourished in the Arab world, had been practically nonexistent in Europe.

ENTER SCIENCE

When science began to re-emerge in the 1500's, it began by observing and describing the outer, visible universe. It did this because this was an area free from the influence of the Church. The laws of nature were not subject to Papal edict.

The Renaissance scientists, who considered themselves natural philosophers, were interested in getting real answers to real mysteries. They were inspired by the ancient Greeks who examined the world and held discourse on the nature of things. It was not enough for these scientists to know that the perfect pattern was held in the Mind of God. They wanted to know, themselves, the Truths of Nature, so they concentrated their investigations on that which was visible and self evident before them - the earth, the sky, the sea, and all things within it. At the same time, they had a deep reverence for that which exists beyond the reach of the senses. Nature was seen as a reflection, in solid form, of forces that extended beyond the physical plane. In this respect, natural philosophy resonated with the ancient Greeks who taught that aside from practical considerations, profound wisdom and meaning could be derived from studying the shape(s) of Nature.

The newly-awakening power of observation and analysis quickly changed the mental landscape of the time. Copernicus proposed that the earth and planets moved around the sun, a direct blow to the church doctrine that the earth was at the center of the universe. Kepler followed with his theories of planetary motion. Galileo's telescopic discoveries and observations of falling bodies, motion and inertia laid the groundwork for Newton, who defined the concepts of the forces of gravity and motion as they appear from a three-dimensional perspective, and placed them within the framework of absolute space and time.

Within 200 years after Luther nailed his protest to the cathedral doors, the foundation of a new description was firmly in place. Newton was the father of classical physics and astronomy, and his view of the visible universe dominated science for over two hundred years. The world view that evolved from this description still dominates western culture.

The underlying assumption of this view was that the world *out there* represents an objective, stable reality that exists independently of anyone's observation and/or participation. Objects in that reality were carefully studied and measured and found to act consistently throughout time and space, but as the incredible precision governing the material world became more evident, more complex, the precision itself became the focus. The material effects of reality were more immediate to the senses than the invisible Source of reality, and so there developed the vision of a great clockwork universe with planets going around in their orbits, with every effect having a previous cause in time, and with every action causing an equal and opposite reaction. Life, the great Causative Principle, became almost incidental to the overall picture.

This viewpoint became known as Material Determinism. The extreme position of this philosophy claimed that if the state of every particle in the universe could be known for any given moment, then the entire past and future of the cosmos could be worked out for all time. Free will was thought to be nonexistent. All conscious choice was seen as being determined by external or material conditions. Without a consciously developed avenue for the influx of Spirit, Life was seen to be blindly playing out a predetermined course set in motion in the far distant past.

Toward the end of the 19th Century, science expressed all this and more in the 2nd Law of Thermodynamics which stated that entropy (the movement from order to disorder) is irreversible, that the Universe is moving inexorably toward an eventual heat death in which all the stored up energy of the stars and galaxies will have been dissipated into space.

By consciously choosing to study the material, earth appearance (the visible effects of reality) while ignoring the invisible (causes of reality), science created a closed perceptual loop within which it operated. Classical scientific knowledge developed within the boundaries of this closed system for nearly five hundred years. It increased the power of vision through telescopes and microscopes and explored everything in sight, but when it reached the theoretical limits of seeing, ie. the boundary of the physical world, it found itself in a philosophical vacuum, knowing the *how* of everything and the *why* of nothing.

The key to resolving the despair implicit in the Second Law is to realize that it applies only within a closed system. The determinist view simply assumed that our visible system of stars and galaxies had been wound up by the Creator and then left to wind down, to expend its allotted sum of energy and then die.

In an open system, energy flows through, and all forms of mineral and crystal, all species of plant, animal and human, from simple to complex, grow and develop through the use of energy that is freely available to all. As forms die or wear away, new ones take their places. Our entire system is Self-renewing and Self-sustaining. In contrast to this, the Second Law of Thermodynamics illustrates the complete denial of the Creative Principle, and the extent to which classical science had isolated humanity from the Source of power.

About this time, the end of the 19th Century, some scientists were beginning to think everything in physics was known or could be discovered by using known principles. Although this sounds absurd today, the truth is that the major discoveries of the Newtonian era were complete, and physics was either at an end or on the threshold of a new description of reality.

PROBABILITY FACTORS

The revolution in physics in the 20th Century began to show the paths that were now opening up in science. As physicists explored the invisible world of atomic and subatomic particles, they discovered that Newton's neatly packaged description of the physical universe was unravelling. One major strand that unravelled was the premise that everything could be learned through direct observation of the physical world.

In the new physics, quantum physics, direct observation of matter was impossible, since the atomic structure of matter could not be seen but only deduced from observation of effects produced. In addition, as scientists began to formulate an image of the atom, they found that though certain elements of the structure were clear, others were indeterminate.

In the early 20th Century, the existence of the electron was known and its orbits, or states had been calculated, but no one had ever seen one, and there was no way to isolate one for study. In 19th Century classical mechanics, an object was subjected to various measurements to determine its mass, position, velocity and momentum in order to arrive at an understanding of the forces involved in its motion. Though atomic particles were thought of as objects similar to tiny billiard balls, when scientists tried to calculate their exact properties they found that there was an inherent limit on the accuracy they could achieve. The closer they got to an exact measurement of one property, the farther they got from any knowledge of its other properties. If velocity were measured to any degree of accuracy, position would become proportionately more uncertain. If the position of a particle were measured with total precision, the velocity (or direction of travel) would become completely unknown.

The result was that in order to maintain accuracy in description, scientists had to describe atomic and subatomic particles as groups, streams in motion. Individual particles could only be described in terms of *probabilities* rather than in statements of exact certainty.

This was truly a revolution in the way that we described our world. In Newtonian physics there was no room for probabilities: a thing was or it wasn't. Now Pandora's box had been opened, for if an event has only a high probability of occurring in a certain way, it means that in principle, the probability exists for it to occur in *all other ways* as well. All that is required for a probability to become a likelihood is a different perspective, a different *point of view.*

The prospect of radically different perspectives emerged in the early 1900's with Einstein's theories of relativity. Few people, then or now, understand all the ramifications of these new ideas. Certainly it was recognized by some that the structure of the world as it had been known and described in classical physics was gone forever. Absolute space and time, the Newtonian concept that space was the same in every direction and time ran at the same rate throughout the universe, were replaced by the concept of an elastic, four-dimensional space-time continuum.

In relativity, the gravitational fields associated with massive bodies such as stars and planets have the effect of curving space-time, and this means that light will not always travel in a straight line. In a curved space, Euclidean geometry no longer applies: a triangle can have more than 180 degrees, parallel lines can and do meet, and a straight line is no longer the shortest distance between two points.

One of the mind-stretching concepts of relativity is that space and time are flexible. High-speed travel and strong gravitational fields can slow down time, and an object that is moving very rapidly is observed to be shorter than the same object that is not moving, relative to the observer. The key point is the word "relative." In other words, the observer travelling along with the object, at the same speed will not measure any shortening because her rulers will also be shortened in proportion to the speed of travel. Only someone at rest in relation to the moving object can measure the shortening effect.

These distortions of time and space get more pronounced the faster the speed, so that at the speed of light (the fastest speed there is), time stops completely. A particle of light that travels across the vast reaches of space (at the speed of light, of course) is said to have taken billions of light years to reach our planet, but, for the beam of light, the passage of time does not exist. From its own perspective, the particle of light (the photon) is everywhere along its journey at the same time.

In the Newtonian world view, an event was thought to appear the same way to every observer; ie. the motion of a ball rolling down the same inclined plane under the same conditions would always move at the same rate, no matter who was making the observation. Now, in the world view according to relativity, the "same event" can and does appear differently to observers who are in different frames of reference, who perceive the event from a different perspective or point of view. This was not how science had come to perceive the world and some members of the scientific community found this and other aspects of relativity unsettling. Many features of relativity run counter to "common sense," but as Einstein once remarked, common sense is simply a body of prejudice built up in the mind by the time a person reaches the age of eighteen.

Once quantum theory and relativity became established, the scientific basis for the familiar common sense view of objects interacting in space and time was forever altered. Quantum theory tells us that solid objects are made up primarily of vast empty spaces and that when we observe the widely separated sub-atomic particles that presumably constitute the solidity of an object, they can show up as matter in the form of particles (atoms, protons, electrons, etc.) or as energy in the form of waves (electromagnetic radiation), depending upon how the observation is set up. Scientists studying the subatomic structure of physical substance have found that when they set up their experimental apparatus to observe particles, they find particles, but when the equipment is configured to look for waves, the substance is observed in the form of energy waves. Relativity tells us that matter (the particle) and energy (the wave) are one thing and that they are interchangeable. This is the famous particle-wave duality that has mys-tified science in the 20th Century.

In the description of the subatomic structure of physical matter by the founders of quantum mechanics, the <u>observation</u> of a particle is what brings that particle into "existence." Until a conscious entity makes the observation of a particle of physical matter, its material existence is only a probability. In other words, that substance could take form as a particle, or it could take form as a wave. No one can say which it will be until the observation is made. The kicker is that the observer determines what form will appear by the way the experiment is configured. Look for particles and one must find particles - look for waves and inevitably one finds waves.

Due to these and other fascinating experiments, some scientists now speculate that the *intent* and the *actions* of the *observer* are the *determining fac-tor* in causing energy to appear in one form or another. The extension of this principle into everyday life is that our personal reality takes shape around us according to our *intent* and our *definitions of what is possible or likely*. This is a concept that empowers each of us to bring into existence the life experience of our own choosing.

We truly create our own reality by the way we <u>choose</u> to
perceive the energy that surrounds us.

If an event occurs in a different way for each observer depending upon the individual *point of view* (or frame of reference), then each different observation of the "same event" is equally valid. In such a system the focus shifts from the <u>event</u> to the <u>observer of the event</u>. This leads to the conclusion that truth is not objective, ie. *proceeding from the object known*; rather, truth is subjective, *pro-ceeding from the subject, knowing*. The result of these developments is to place each individual consciousness in direct relation to the entire cosmos.

Considering all this, there can be no objective standard that determines which of our perceptions are valid and which are invalid. The appearances of the phenomenal world seem to be consistent because we have been trained since birth to agree that they are. For instance, we agree that the world is solid even though scientists tell us that solidity is an illusion: matter = empty space. Knowing this, we must consider the possibility that if we could dissolve the agreement that the world is as it appears, then in theory, or in actuality (as don Juan teaches), the familiar world would dissolve and another would take its place.

This may seem to be an extreme view, but this happens every time we learn something new. The world based on the old view collapses and is replaced by a new world. It all happens so seamlessly that we seldom notice that we constantly create our world anew, moment to moment.

AS WE ACTIVELY REDEFINE OUR REALITY, WE RECREATE IT.

We change our point of view and the world of appearances, of events and circumstances, shifts to reflect the changes we are making at an internal level.

This is the essence of THE EXPERIMENT. It is an experiment that we perform on ourselves. Throughout this book and in the books to follow, our teachers take us on a series of "strolls" around what they call the *concept pool,* an archetypal pool of ideas from which we may draw. We are encouraged to open our minds to this flow of ideas and to consider new and sometimes very different ways of interpreting reality. As we develop new mental pathways, our expanded awareness reflects onto the earth stage as a richer, fuller personal existence, one that is more closely aligned with the beneficent forces of the Cosmos.

PERCEPTION AND FOCUS

The subtitle of this book is "an exploration of perception and focus," and the next sections, *Light and Color,* and *Sound and Music,* begin to describe the mechanisms we use to see and hear, but not just in terms of retina and eardrum. Earth existence, as we experience it, narrowly defines the limits of our perception, and our collective focus has been trained to see and hear certain things with great clarity, and to ignore others.

We can hear and acknowledge the voices of others around us, but when it comes to voices we hear in our heads, the silent, inner voices, we are often told that these are suspect. In some circles, they might be called the voices of temptation, or of the devil; in others, hearing voices is a sign of mental instability: those who claim to hear the voice of God are often considered unbalanced. For one reason or another, many of us are taught to mistrust and ignore those inner voices, and yet learning to distinguish the Inner Voice of the Teacher from the ego-based, "small me" chatter of a cluttered mind, is one of the most challenging and rewarding tasks we can accomplish. The challenge is to reach a place of deep, inner silence, and that takes patient and persistent practice. The reward is that by making contact with our Teacher, we open a channel to a guide whose wisdom and understanding is always present, throughout our lives.

Our sense of vision is also tightly focused. We are well-trained (and quite comfortable) at seeing the world of solid objects, but start talking about seeing something that "isn't there" and people will begin to edge away, casting sideways glances at you while whispering amongst themselves. Yet Inner Vision, like the Inner Voice, is our conscious connection to a vast store of knowledge that exists within us and around us, invisible, but real. As we will see in the section on Light, the light energy we see is a minute fraction of the light energy that we know is around us, and the light energy we know of is a minute fraction of the energy of the cosmos. As we progress into the New Age and the new millennium, our adventure, as explorers, is to bring what is now the unknown into the realm of the known. We do this, not by going beyond our senses, but by going beyond the boundaries we have set upon our senses, to claim what is rightfully ours. As a line in THE EXPERIMENT says,

"We must see the unseen, and hear the unheard,
to know the unknown."

Although this may sound slightly esoteric, it has a lot to do with practical everyday matters. Our original premise was that since birth, most of us in western society have been trained to think of the visible world of appearances as the primary focus and the invisible world as belonging to the area of religion or philosophy, or even superstition, but in THE EXPERIMENT, the invisible side of reality is the area where events in the physical world first begin to take shape. As we become aware of the interplay between visible and invisible, we can begin to join in shaping our world rather than being at the mercy of event and circumstance.

This is where the practical work of THE EXPERIMENT begins. In a world view where the visible world predominates and the invisible is hidden, events appear to come out of nowhere, sometimes dealing out unpleasant surprises. In view of this, it helps to expand our world view to include knowledge of the invisible. When we do this, through methods that we will touch on in this book, information begins to flow to us from these invisible sources. And, while limitation is one of the key aspects of visible reality, the invisible world, by contrast, is limitless. By incorporating ideas from the *concept pool* into our mental landscapes, we extend those landscapes to include the inner, invisible layers of reality that have such a strong influence on the events that unfold in the physical world.

We can develop the ability to move across the boundaries that have traditionally separated these layers and learn to act in both visible and invisible fields of focus. As we do this, we gradually incorporate the two sides into a unified field of awareness, and we achieve a state of consciousness that allows the limitless power of the Cosmos to flow into and shape the events of our lives. The shape of those events will depend upon our personal predilictions, our personal goals and aspirations, but every one who takes these steps will find their personal lives enhanced with beauty, harmony, inspiration and love.

The first step is to develop an awareness of the invisible layers around us and begin to see how they interact with the visible layers. THE EXPERIMENT speaks of this duality in terms of <u>*Reflector*</u> and <u>*reflection.*</u> The *reflection* (small "r") is everything that is visible to the eye and available to the physical senses. The *Reflector* (capital "R") is the invisible energy source that surrounds us, creates us and supports us. Some call it the SOURCE, THE ALL, ALL THAT IS, or THE FORCE, but whatever the name, IT is the origin of all worlds, visible and invisible.

This duality is presented in terms of *Reflector* and *reflection* to point out some particular qualities. Imagine walking in the mountains and seeing the reflection of a tree in a still pool of water. We regard the reflection as a fleeting image, an illusion. If we walk on and change our angle of perception, the image changes and then disappears, to be replaced by other images. The reality (we think) is the tree itself, the source of the reflection. The same is true when we see our own reflection in a mirror. We think of ourselves as real and the reflection as an illusion. When we turn from the mirror, our image disappears. The mirror itself is neutral, reflecting whatever is in view and what we see in it depends upon our angle to the mirror.

The teachers in THE EXPERIMENT tell us that the medium in which we exist is reflective, like a mirror, and that our surroundings and our experiences are the way we perceive aspects of the boundless energy of the *Reflector*, reflecting ITSELF into form. In fact, they often refer to our earth experience as a mirror, or as the *reflection*. Imagine that "reality" is layered and that each alternate layer of reality is also a reflection of the energy of the *Reflector*, THE ALL. THE EXPERIMENT describes the differences that separate one layer from another as differences in the angle from which each one perceives the energy of the *Reflector*. Here on earth, in our reality, we walk past a mirror or a pool of still water and as we move, ie. *change our angle of perception*, the images we see change. Apply the same principle on a larger level, and there can be an infinite number of layers, each one existing at a different angle in relation to the *Reflector*, each one experiencing a distinctly unique reality.

On the earth stage we share a common angle that allows us to experience the group reality of land and sea and sky, of plants and animals, but within this group focus, angle variation can produce different effects. The changing angles of the earth to the sun produce the changes in the seasons. The greater the angle, the greater the difference between seasons. At the equator, where the changes in angles are slight, the seasons hardly vary. At the poles, the angle variation is so extreme that winter brings eternal night, and summer brings eternal day. The changing angles between the sun, moon and earth produce the ebb and flow of the tides.

The limitations we experience on earth such as gravity or time are large-scale features of the *reflection*. But throughout our stories of existence on earth, individuals and groups have always attempted to make *variations* that would help us transcend the limitations that seem to come with the territory. The mastery of fire allowed us to move into the more temperate zones on the earth's surface. Learning to grow our own food gave us a stability that allowed us to develop higher forms of consciousness. Developments like these broadened the general angle of perception and opened new layers, previously invisible layers, for exploration and use.

Imagine the excitement of the first person to get up on a horse's back and travel in an hour what would previously have taken a day. Now, with our modern airplanes, we have escaped from the limitation of gravity itself, and in a few hours we can complete a journey that once took months. This power has integrated widely separated lands and brought what was unknown and mysterious into everyday usage.

Now, in the new millennium and the New Age, we are on the threshhold of new boundaries, ready to demolish even greater limitations. As one segment of adventurers pushes off into outer space, the newest territory awaiting us is inner space, inner mental universes, and the techniques in THE EXPERIMENT will help those of us who are bold enough and adventurous enough to travel through invisible layers of reality, and like the explorers of old, to return with tales of wonder and endless opportunity. Each boundary that we cross, each previously invisible layer that we explore brings us excitement and wonder, and the knowledge we gain enlarges us all. Best of all, our explorations do not require a government grant or billions of dollars. They require only that we use the abilities inherent within us. By drawing from the concept pool and by following the simple exercises with color, sound and creative visualization, each of us will learn to build our own inner spaceship and begin to travel the highways of inner space.

Does this sound extreme or far-out? It isn't! We each have our deepest held hopes and dreams, and inner space travel is the surest way to reach them. At any given moment, we exist on one layer of reality and our goals or our aspirations exist on other layers. Traditionally, one way to move through the layers is to persist in time. A child says, "I wish I was a grown-up so I could be my own boss." In time, the child grows up and realizes that goal. Many of us take a similar approach to our goals, ie., "keep on keepin' on, and hope for the best." By learning inner space travel we can accelerate our movement through the layers that separate us from the fulfilment of our desires. As we begin our first, tentative explorations, we open layers within us that expand our awareness of who we are and what we can accomplish. As we proceed, we gain confidence because we find that seemingly insurmountable obstacles on the visible, physical side dissolve when we work from within the inner invisible side.

This is the practical side of inner space travel and it is based on a well-established mathematical principle: barriers that exist in one dimension are easily overcome by simply moving into a higher dimension. There is a 19th Century fable called <u>Flatland</u> about a flat, two-dimensional reality inhabited by imaginary beings of the type that could be drawn on a piece of paper - figures such as squares, circles and triangles. They move around on their flat-plane reality and when two shapes meet, they can go around each other and on their way. However, when one of these shapes meets a line extending across its path of travel, the line is an impenetrable barrier. In Flatland, the concept of over or under simply does not exist, and so the line cannot be crossed.

To three-dimensional beings, such as ourselves, the line is not a limit. We simply step over it. The barrier in two dimensions disappears for those in three dimensions. Inner space travel works in the same way to overcome the barriers we encounter in our progression through three-dimensional space-time earth reality. As we practice the techniques in THE EXPERIMENT, drawing ideas from the concept pool, working the color experiments, living with the color charts and building the inner spaceship, we develop the mental flexibility to extend into dimensions of thought and imagination beyond the third dimension. We learn to forge alternate pathways that take us around, or through, or over the obstacles that used to block us.

As long as we consider the external, sensory layers of experience to be the only, or even the principal reality, we are like the prisoners of the cave, and we remain, to a certain extent, at the mercy of events and circumstances. When we begin to operate consciously in the invisible layers of reality, we take our rightful place in the cosmos as creators, shapers of reality. Whether we work toward achieving our goals or simply go in for exploration, inner space travel is challenging, fun and exciting. There are layers within us to be discovered and worlds that lie hidden behind the visible fabric of the outer world. These worlds are real, and they await us.

To open and prepare us for our journey, THE EXPERIMENT gives us a powerful set of tools using color and sound to help us see the duality of *Reflector* and *reflection*. In the next two sections, we look at some aspects of our perception of color and sound that are often ignored. It sometimes gets a bit technical, but if you bear with us, we can lay a foundation for the material that follows in CHAPTER ONE, STARTING WITH EVERYTHING, as well as providing an introduction to the color charts of the keys of music.

While THE EXPERIMENT was being written, the teachers instructed us in making a series of color charts based on mathematical and musical patterns of harmony. They told us that living with these charts, or paintings, was an important element in producing the changes that would lead us to a closer alignment with the invisible forces that nourish and shape our world. Just as eating good, healthy food nourishes the physical body, looking at the patterns in the color charts feeds the eye and begins to align the electromagnetic cellular structure of the body to a larger pattern of order and harmony.

This concept of alignment may seem abstract, but we only need to look around us to see how important it is. Consider a radio. If the dial isn't precisely aligned with the station we want, the reception will be fuzzy, distorted. The same is true with precision instruments; when aligned they give an accurate reading; when misaligned, they become useless. When human personality is aligned with the harmonious patterns of the Cosmos, the energy of SUPER-consciousness flows smoothly through our personal vehicles to create harmonious reflections on our earth stage.

So we set to work making the charts, and soon they were all around us, covering the walls and even some of the ceilings. We lived with and worked with the charts for some time. Then one day we woke up, looked around, and realized that everything was different. The furniture had changed, we had achieved a relaxed sense of prosperity in our business, the tensions and stresses of life had mellowed or melted away; our whole lives and surroundings had shifted without our really noticing. Our teachers laughed and said that that was the effect of alignment - subtle, at first, but unmistakable. And so we were launched on our course. . .

THE EXPERIMENT actually begins with a music chart, and CHAPTER ONE, STARTING WITH EVERYTHING, uses the chart and our perception of light and color to introduce the concepts that will take the reader, like Alice in <u>Through The Looking Glass</u>, into vast new fields of knowledge and experience

on the other side of the mirror.

LIGHT AND COLOR

We all have the potential within us to step through reality's looking glass, but what exactly does that mean? We are surrounded and in some sense, hemmed in, by our beliefs about ourselves, who we think we are, what we think we deserve, and all of this gets reinforced by what we <u>see</u> around us. We may look at our car and think, "If I were more successful, I'd drive a nicer car, but I really can't afford it." Or someone might look around at his/her office cubicle and say, "Boy, I'd love to get out of here and be my own boss." Perhaps some of us are thinking, "I know that there is more to reality than what I see, but how do I break through the appearances of reality to see and experience the larger view?"

The problem is that the world of appearances presents a seamless continuity to one's perception: what you see today is what you'll probably be seeing tomorrow. And seeing something is usually considered proof that it's real, that it exists.

But what if we all knew that what we **see** is only half the picture?

Things could be quite different.

Try this simple color experiment:

 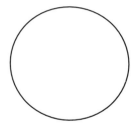

Look at the red circle under a bright light for thirty seconds. Hold the page about twelve to fifteen inches from your eyes and gaze fixedly at the color without looking around. Then look at the blank circle or just close your eyes.

What is going on here? Why does the eye see green in the blank circle after looking at red? Color theorists will say that this is the phenomenon of SUC-CESSIVE CONTRAST though that doesn't really explain anything. Scientists often call this effect "retinal fatigue," a strange term since this effect is most pronounced upon waking when the eyes are completely refreshed.

This effect of seeing what many call an "afterimage" is something we all experience every moment of our waking lives. Everything we look at, however briefly, produces this effect, although it usually goes unnoticed. We tend to think of it as something unimportant, perhaps as an amusement for children, but in THE EXPERIMENT, this visual anomaly is the key to a door that leads us into an invisible, hidden side of reality.

"And what," you may ask, "does looking at red and seeing green have to do with my car, or my job, or my dream of widening my perception?"

The puzzle of the color experiment brings up a question that philosophers and scientists in all ages have struggled with, the question of how to resolve the conflict of opposites and contradictions that seems to be an inescapable part of life on earth, or of perception in three dimensions.

To answer that it may be helpful to go back to a time when Europe was locked in the grip of the dark ages, to the year 1200 AD, to the city of Fez, near Alexandria in North Africa. While much of Europe was languishing in ignorance and superstition, the Arab world, stimulated by the Golden Age of Greece, had become a center of learning. The library at Alexandria was said to have been vast: a collection of the wisdom of the greatest minds in philosophy, mathematics, metaphysics, science and the arts.

In Fez at this time, a group of philosophers, alchemists, astrologers and mages from around the world had gathered to encode their secret wisdom into a system of visual images. The work that grew out of this gathering became known as Tarot. The images in the cards were designed to recall from our subconscious memory the knowledge of how to develop our personalities into vehicles for the beneficent forces of the Cosmos and thus achieve our heart's desires.

Tarot is a lifetime study but one of the images has a lot to do with our color experiment. The card numbered 12, called The Hanged Man, pictures a person hanging upside down from a gallows. The outward appearance is that he is in danger, and yet his expression is serene and his white hair is suggestive of a halo, indicating a state of enlightenment. How do we resolve this image? In the symbolic language of Tarot, the gallows is in a shape that represents THE ALL, ALL THAT IS, the FORCE. This suggests that we must give up our reliance on outer appearances and grow to depend upon an inner force that shapes, harmonizes and <u>supports</u> the outer world. One of the key words associated with this image is *reversal*. The lesson is that by seeing or experiencing the opposites in any situation we can achieve balance and stability.

What you see right before your eyes is but one aspect of life; what is hidden or invisible to the eyes is another side. The way we look and see the color red is how we perceive the visible universe. The green afterimage, its opposite, is a clue that an invisible world exists, contained, but hidden, within the visible, available to senses that are mostly ignored or dismissed. The two worlds, visible and invisible together, create THE WHOLE, THE ONE, THE ALL, and we need to unite these worlds to take our rightful place among the stars.

It is the purpose of THE EXPERIMENT to open our eyes and our senses to an invisible world, to integrate invisible with visible so we can begin to *see* the whole picture instead of the half view that we have come to know as "reality."

Color is a logical pathway toward this resolution because color crosses the boundaries we are looking to dissolve. If our sense of vision is the "prison house" mentioned in Plato's Cave analogy, then color is the wall that we are forced to gaze at, for just as the prisoners of the cave were chained so that the only thing they could see was the wall with the flickering images, so we are chained by the mechanics of vision so that the only thing we can see is color. Look around. Everything presents itself to us as color. The incredible details we see, the nuances of shape and form are all due to differences in color and shading.

Without getting too deeply into the intricacies of color theory let's take a closer look at color. Color is the visible portion of light/energy. Science has mapped out a range of light from the low frequency radio waves that stretch out over several kilometers, to the incredibly high frequency bursts of energy known as cosmic rays, or gamma rays. In between are the various light frequencies familiar to us: electrical power, telephone, microwave, heat energy, ultraviolet and x rays. All these forms of energy are light, but right between infrared (heat energy) and ultraviolet light is a tiny segment of frequencies known as white, or visible, light. This is the light that we see by.

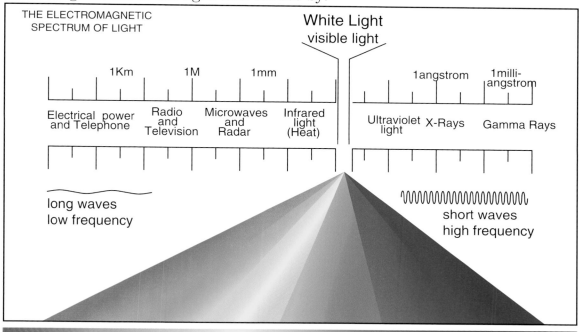

THE ELECTROMAGNETIC SPECTRUM OF LIGHT

White Light
visible light

1Km   1M   1mm   1angstrom   1milli-angstrom

Electrical power and Telephone   Radio and Television   Microwaves and Radar   Infrared light (Heat)   Ultraviolet light   X-Rays   Gamma Rays

long waves low frequency

short waves high frequency

THE SOLAR SPECTRUM   THE HUES OF VISIBLE LIGHT

The range of light in the electromagnetic spectrum is truly vast. If you measure it in octaves, it is over sixty octaves between the lowest and highest frequency waves. Each octave is double the frequency of the preceding one. When a number is doubled sixty times, the result is an astronomically large number. Then consider that the visible light energy that illuminates our reality is but one octave in this incredible range of energy and we get an inkling of how narrowly defined our visible world is, or, by contrast, how vast is the range of that which is invisible.

It is worth noting here an aspect of visible light: it is, in one important respect, invisible. Consider the following contradiction. When we look at a radiant source of light (a star, a light bulb) we see light directly, but when we look away, the light becomes invisible even though it is all around us. Look across the room. You don't see the light in the air - you look right through it - it's invisible. (The astronauts' experiences in outer space have demonstrated this. When they look toward the sun they see light, but when they look away, they experience the utter blackness of space because, although they are surrounded by sunlight, there is nothing out there to reflect it to the eye and render it visible.) Visible light becomes visible when it is reflected from the surface of an object to reach the eye as color.

Color is contained within light as shown by Isaac Newton's famous experiment. He passed a beam of sunlight through a prism and separated it into the colors of the solar spectrum just as raindrops do in creating the effect of a rainbow. This process, called refraction, shows all the colors of visible light.

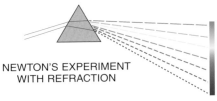

NEWTON'S EXPERIMENT
WITH REFRACTION

Reflection, the process by which we <u>see</u> the color of an object, works differently. The light that shines upon an object within our view contains all the colors of the spectrum, but we don't see objects as being rainbow colored. The things we see have a unique color or combination of colors. The scientific explanation tells us that every object has pigments on its surface, material that reacts to visible light by absorbing some frequencies of color and reflecting others. The colors the pigment absorbs are invisible to the eye, and the colors it reflects are visible.

However, to explain our perception of color only in terms of pigments would be to turn something truly mysterious into something ordinary. We would be falling into the trap of thinking we understand something that we can really only describe. So, let us just say that everything that appears on this earth interacts with the visible spectrum in a way that causes certain colors to be visible and others to be invisible.

Consider, for a moment, the Eastern concept that everything we see is illusion, *maya*. Then consider the scientific finding that all matter is essentially empty space - that solidity is an illusion.

Now consider a curious statement. If we look up the word "color" in the dictionary, alongside the familiar concepts of hue, brightness, saturation, etc., one definition of color is "an appearance, a semblance, a pretense, a disguise." Here we have three different sources all telling us that what we see is an illusion, a disguise. But we are also taught, if we study Eastern philosophy, or Alchemy, or Ageless Wisdom, that within any illusion lies the key to resolving it and solving the puzzle.

And what is the essence of the puzzle? It is the illusion of separateness- the separation that divides us from each other, from our Source and from the object world. We live in a world of sharp distinctions. We all have separate bodies, and all the objects around us appear to have distinct boundaries where they begin and end. Yet science has found that everything within the range of our perception is made of the same elements, and that these elements all have their origin from one thing. The philosophies mentioned before tell us the same: that all things are from ONE.

Overcoming the illusion of separateness is known by alchemists and philosophers who study the hidden mysteries as the greatest challenge to perception, and the way we see color is both the cause of the illusion and a clue to its potential solution.

This brings us back to our color experiment.

The light that shines on this page has all the visible colors in it, but the only color we see when we look at the experiment is red. The rest of the colors remain hidden, invisible. But when we gaze for a while on the color red - we see green. Is the green in the red? Where, exactly, does it come from? It seems to be an intimation from the invisible side that the separation between visible and invisible is an illusion. It is a hint that comes from the mechanism that makes the illusion seem real in the first place, our sense of vision.

I must confess to feeling like one of the prisoners of the cave, trying to convince the others that there is a whole world of light and movement, of sound and color, behind us, just out of sight. When all the evidence of our senses tells us that the world we see is real and complete in itself, it takes a piece of evidence that doesn't quite fit, combined with a curious mind, to begin to break down the illusion.

The little piece of evidence we offer is the afterimage, but to explain what it does, we need a little color theory. Appendix C goes into the formation of the artist's color wheel in some detail. Here we'll just look at the relationship of opposite, or complementary colors.

> The color system we're describing is the one a painter uses in mixing colors, the *subtractive* system. For more on *subtractive* vs *additive* color perception, see Appendix B, p.192.

Red and green are one pair of opposite colors. Every hue the eye can see has its own, unique, complementary opposite which can be found by simply looking at the color. Gaze at a color, and the afterimage that emerges is the opposite, or complementary color. How does this show us the invisible side?

We know from our experiment that any glimpse of the world around us splits the spectrum of colors into the ones we see, and the ones we don't. We look out over a beautiful landscape. The sky may be intensely blue, but hidden within that blue is an equally intense orange, the opposite of blue. The emerald green of the sun-drenched hills conceals a beautiful hue of red. Within the violet of the distant mountains there lies a brilliant yellow, waiting to be discovered. Can we see these other colors? Yes. If we look long enough at anything or any color, we will see the afterimage, but the key to understanding the implications of this effect is to look at how color works.

Let's use a simple color wheel to see the relations between the colors. The colors across from each other are pairs of opposites. The green is across from the red, orange is across from blue, and violet is across from yellow. Leaving out, for now, the mystical seventh color, indigo, we can see that the basic color wheel of six colors represents a simplified, or schematic, solar spectrum.

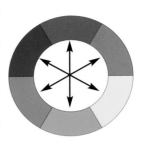

The arrangement of the wheel also shows something about how opposite colors are related. Green is the opposite of red and it lies directly across the wheel from red, but we also know (from the crayon school of color theory) that green is a mixture of yellow and blue, and on the wheel, it is positioned between those two colors. The same goes for the other opposites. Orange is across from blue and sits between red and yellow, the two colors that mix to create it. Violet is across from yellow, its opposite, and between red and blue, its two component colors.

Notice that of the six colors on the wheel above, three of them (orange, green and violet) are mixtures of the other three colors, red, yellow and blue. There is another wheel (at left) that picks up the hues between the six colors, giving us red-orange, yellow orange, yellow green, etc. for a total of twelve hues, but whether we have six, twelve or an infinite number of hues, they all reduce to the same three colors, red, yellow and blue. These colors, which painters know as the primary colors, cannot be reduced to any mixture - they are pure hues of color and, as such, they represent the essential colors in the system of pigments that gives each object its color.

We've mentioned that pairs of opposite colors are also known as complementary colors. In the dictionary, a *complement* is defined as that which completes, or makes whole. In color theory, an individual color and its complement, form one, complete unit. Let's see how this works out in practice.

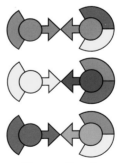

Red is a pure tone. It contains not a trace of the other colors, yellow or blue. Its complementary color, green, is a mixture that contains only yellow and blue. If we separate green into its component parts, we could just as well say that the opposite of red is yellow and blue. Similarly, the opposite of yellow is red and blue (violet). The opposite of blue is red and yellow (orange). In this way, each color and its complement together make up the whole spectrum of color. Remember that the essence of the spectrum is red, yellow and blue.

Now we begin to see something about how our perception of color can resolve the illusion of separateness. When we look at yellow, for instance, the light shining on that color has, within it, all the hues of color, but because of the limitations of vision, we see only yellow. The other colors of the spectrum (red and blue) have been somehow separated from view. But when we gaze at yellow, the afterimage shows us violet, a mixture of red and blue. So the sight of yellow brings together red and blue to complete the spectrum by supplying the missing colors. This may seem like a subtle point, but it deals a devastating blow to the idea that the world consists of separate, individual objects.

First, consider that when we see an individual color, the source of that specific color is all color. Why? Because the visible light that illuminates what we see contains all the colors of the spectrum. When we look at something, the eye/brain connection separates the one from the whole - we then appear to see the specific color as being distinct, or separate, from the whole spectrum of colors. Our brief look at color has shown us a principle at work - that for vision, at least, *the whole is the origin of the specific* .

Then consider what happens when we look at the specific color. That same eye/brain connection that makes the separation, then produces the afterimage to remind us that the separation is an illusion. The specific comes from the whole and also leads us back to the whole.

We have used the experiments to bring the perception to a narrow focus, to illustrate a point about how we see our world. Now expand back into normal perception and realize that for everything we see, the eye/brain mechanism produces an afterimage of its exact complement. We don't generally notice that this is happening, but our entire visual life experience simultaneously registers as its opposite and complement.

If we use our experience with color to illustrate a larger principle, we can say that the sense of separation that exists between ourselves and the rest of the world can be understood in terms of the lessons of color. First, nothing exists in isolation. Everything that appears separate comes from the WHOLE. Secondly, everything that appears separate has a marker within it that points up the underlying unity. In other words, the WHOLE is the origin of its parts.

All things come from the ONE.

THE EXPERIMENT is a series of strolls around the *concept pool* and as we stroll, we sample ideas from varying angles of perception. Some of us dive in and swim, some of us stoop to drink, but whatever our style, the ideas we take in become a part of our mental landscape.

The reader may be thinking, "I read the color theory and I tried the experiment. I understand in theory how the invisible world is linked to the visible, but I haven't a clue as to how to see what's invisible."

Awareness grows over time - it doesn't happen on demand. All we need to do at a conscious level is to make accurate observations, provide ourselves with the information that there is a larger force at work out there/in here. Then something takes over and makes the connections we don't feel capable of making. It may take a week or a month or a year, but at some point, the strolls around the concept pool coalesce into knowledge and growth.

This way of learning takes away the stress. All we do is stroll, dip into the pool, drink deeply from what resonates with our deepest longings, and then go on. Once the information is in the conscious mind, subconsciousness takes over. It develops the ideas and reflects them back to the conscious level as increased awareness.

SOUND AND MUSIC

The color and music charts in THE EXPERIMENT are combinations of the keys of music with the colors of the color wheel that we examined in the preceding section. The wheel of twelve colors (at left) is often called the Chromatic scale of color. This scale divides the single octave of visible light into twelve equally spaced colors, starting with red and proceeding through violet to red violet. The progression of twelve colors in this wheel has been correlated to the twelve months of the calendar. (see calendars, p. *111*)

The color wheel has also been linked with the twelve tones that make up the Chromatic scale of music, and it is this relationship between color and sound that makes it possible to paint the Keys of music.

We have said earlier that everything in our three-dimensional world is made of light, but the power of formation, the force of creation, is sound. In humans, shaped sound, or speech, is the power to verbalize thought, to bring the archetypal world of idea to bear upon the physical world and thus shape it as we choose.

But what is sound and why is it linked with creative force? Pythagoras, the ancient Greek philosopher, mathematician and mystic proposed the following metaphysical/mathematical explanation. Pythagoras believed, as does modern science, that the language of numbers provides the most fundamental description of the cosmos, and in this spirit, Pythagoreans represented creation as a progression of numbers.

Prior to a cycle of manifestation, the entire potential of creation is contained within a single point, a point of perfect stillness that was known as the number one, the MONAD. The progression from one to two occurs when the MONAD reflects upon its own being, and in that moment of self-reflection, the one becomes two, the self and the observer of the self. It is this act that brings the *potential* for creation into *actuality*. (This ties in deeply with modern quantum mechanics which states that a particle of matter comes into existence only at the moment that it is observed by a conscious entity.)

In the Pythagorean vision, sound and creation are a simultaneous occurrence. Before a cycle of manifestation begins, sound exists only in a latent form, what the Hindus term *shabda Brahman*, the soundless sound. This follows from the logic of numbers. Sound, as we experience it, is a vibration and vibration is an oscillation, meaning, a back and forth movement from one pole to the other. In perfect unity, the MONAD, there is no *other*, hence perfect stillness. But when duality is established through the agency of *reflection*, movement between opposite poles becomes possible and vibration begins. Sound, therefore, is the first emanation from the MONAD, and it is said that this first slow sonorous movement, this primeval vibration, is the agency that brings the world into manifestation.

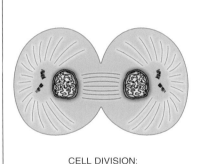

CELL DIVISION:
THE ONE REFLECTS ITSELF INTO TWO

In Pythagorean number mysticism, the number "one" is called the MONAD - it symbolizes the Absolute Unity which contains the infinite possibilities of creation, but there can be no actual creation, no vibration, until the MONAD, *in reflecting upon itself*, initiates the concept of duality. This doubling of One to make two is the first creative act, the original act of reproduction which in all forms of ancient wisdom is described as reflection. Hence it is said that God created man (and everything else) in Its own image because creation is a *reflection* of the One Self into form.

The importance of sound to the Pythagoreans made vibration a principal area of study and their findings became the basis of a system of harmony that is at the core of the western musical tradition. In this tradition, the individual notes are labeled "A" "B" "C" "D" and so on, but Pythagoras found that the note we call "C" is the first audible sound to emerge from the process of vibration. By taking the number two, the origin of vibration, and doubling it repeatedly, one comes to a vibration rate of 16 cycles per second, the rate at which sound becomes audible to the human ear. This sound is the note of C. In India, where the art and science of sound have reached their culmination in the mantra, the sound of this note is called the primal tone from which all sound derives.

We have seen how our perception of color involves an awareness of invisible areas. Our perception of sound does something very similar. The sounds we hear are the audible layer of an ocean of sound that surrounds us.

Consider one of the basic aspects of sound vibration. When a tightly drawn string or a column of air (as a guitar string or an organ pipe) is vibrated, it produces a sound, a tone. This vibration is generally heard by the ear as a single note; in acoustics it is called the fundamental tone. Surrounding this vibrating fundamental tone and *inseparable* from it (as complementary colors are inseparable) is a series of accompanying vibrations called harmonic overtones. (These accompanying, surrounding overtones, or harmonics, although not heard separately, influence and shape the sound that we <u>do</u> hear. This happens to such an extent that instrument makers always experiment with shape and proportion to produce an instrument that emphasizes the harmonics that will sweeten the sound of the tones being played.)

When a string is vibrating, sounding a note, we are hearing the tone (sound wave) corresponding to a vibration of the full length of the string. This is the fundamental tone. At the same time, however, harmonic overtones are being produced as the string <u>spontaneously</u> vibrates in modes that represent one half its length, one third its length, one fourth its length, one fifth its length and so on, perhaps to infinity if our instruments had the sensitivity to perceive it. These naturally occurring harmonic overtones, as the name implies, are tones that harmonize with the fundamental (see following page), and though inaudible, they exist in the chords that compose the major scales or keys of music.

The first harmonic is the fundamental tone C, a vibration of the full length of the string.

The second harmonic is double the frequency, hence C again, since doubling the frequency raises the tone one full octave.

The third harmonic overtone above C is G, a major fifth occurring at three times the frequency of the fundamental.

The fourth harmonic is a doubling of the second, hence produces another C, raised in pitch two octaves above the fundamental.

The fifth harmonic, five times the frequency of the fundamental, produces the note of E, a major third in the key of C-Major.

Thus the first few naturally occurring harmonic overtones of the note of C include the major harmonies (3rd and 5th) in the Key of C Major.

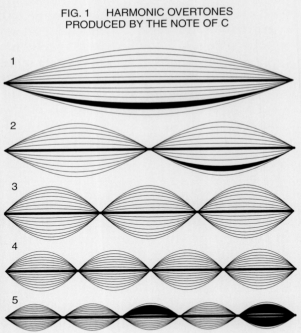

FIG. 1   HARMONIC OVERTONES
PRODUCED BY THE NOTE OF C

The harmonies inherent in sound have been organized, over the centuries, into many patterns. Among the ones that developed in the western musical tradition are the major and minor scales, patterns of tones in an octave that include the major harmonies. The major scale, also called the diatonic scale, is the familiar

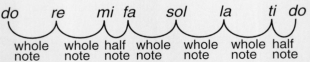

a pattern of tones which traverses an octave of sound in seven steps and returns on the eighth note to the original tone, only raised in pitch by one octave.

The original tone (do) can be any note whatsoever (C, D, E, etc.); it is the structure of the scale that remains the same, half steps between the third and fourth, seventh and eighth notes, whole steps between the other notes. The function of this pattern is to group together the notes within an octave which produce harmonious combinations, whatever the key.

This pattern forms the substructure of the paintings of the keys of music. The music charts are representations, in color, of the harmonic vibrations that sing the cosmos into being.

According to the western system of musical keys, within the first few harmonic overtones of the note of C natural are vibrations that musicians know as the principal harmonies in the C Major scale, the major third and the major fifth (see facing page).

The Cosmos comes into being through the agency of sound, the first audible sound is C, and the vibration that produces the tone of C spontaneously produces the harmonics of G and E, its major harmonious companions. Describing this in words conveys a little but hearing the sound of the chord of C Major, brings home with force the idea that the universe arises in harmony.

THE CHARTS OF THE KEYS OF MUSIC

We have strolled around the concept pool looking at color and sound. We know that seeing a color is a perceptual experience that combines visible (the color) and invisible (the complement) and enables us to reach beyond the separate aspects of existence to glimpse the oneness of all things.

The experience of sound is perhaps a bit more subtle but not less integrating. When we hear a sound, the instrument that gave voice to the vibration (whether it be a human voice or a string plucked or a wind instrument) simultaneously produces a host of harmonic overtones whose inaudible vibrations surround and penetrate our field of awareness by shaping the sound that we do hear. We may not hear the harmonic overtones as separate notes, but without their presence, we would not experience the sounds we do hear in the same way.

The science of acoustics tells us that a sound vibration, like light, is eternal. The sound wave may diminish over time and become inaudible, but it continues to vibrate. (Acoustical engineers speculate that with instruments of increasing capacity, we may be able to recover sound from our distant past, just as our giant telescopes recover the light from distant galaxies that originated, from our perspective, billions of years ago.) The sea of (mostly inaudible) sound that surrounds us stretches back through the dim reaches of time to include the vibrations that formed the cosmos and that continue to shape our world and all that exists. Every sound we hear puts us in touch with the origins of life. Such is the magical power of sound.

In a world where the wonders of technology have made the miraculous seem mundane, we need to reconnect with the SOURCES of life that surround us. Our teachers in THE EXPERIMENT have given us the charts of the musical keys as a tool to help align ourselves with the cosmic forces of harmony. They require no explanation (though we include some for those interested); simply looking at the patterns and colors subtly shifts the energy configuration of the viewer to become more open to the flow of love and harmony that surrounds us.

The correlation between the sounds of music and the colors of the rainbow is a natural one. As vibration increases from inaudible to audible, the first sound that comes into the range of human hearing is the tone of C. As the vibration of electromagnetic energy increases and moves into the visible range, red is the first color that becomes visible to the human eye. By linking C, the first audible tone, with red, the first visible color, we follow an ancient tradition, and a philosophy which holds that the naturally occurring patterns on earth reveal a larger, cosmic Truth.

Following the correlation between sound and color led to the charts of the musical keys and to the beginning of THE EXPERIMENT. The first chart we painted was of the Key of E Major, shown below in a simplified form. This chart is what launches us, in Chapter One, on our journey.

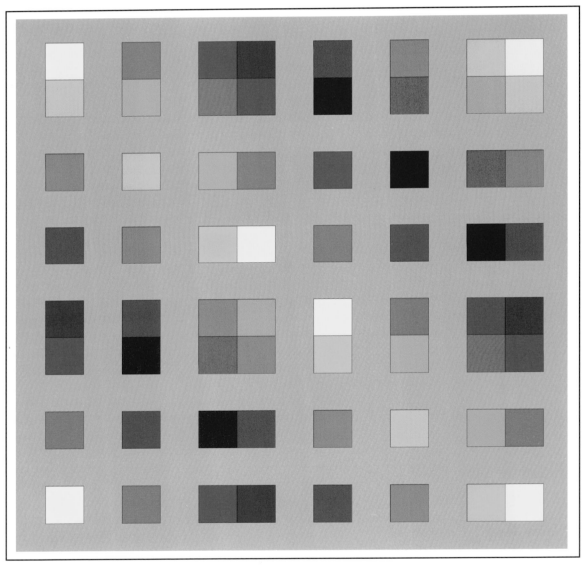

COLOR CHART OF THE KEY OF E MAJOR

AND SO . . .

This brief review of light, color and sound has been included to aid the reader, as many of the premises in THE EXPERIMENT are built on simple facts that we learned in our early school years, and that we take for granted, rarely giving them a second thought. Although we know that our eye reverses all that it sees, we hardly ever stop to think, "Is what I'm seeing really upside down?" or, "Is that red apple really green?" It is because of our ready acceptance of things "as they look" that these rules have been called to our attention once again by the teachers in THE EXPERIMENT. They want us to remember that things are not as they appear, and that often everything is actually the very opposite of the way we see it.

Throughout history, different cultures have had people whose function is to remind everyone that this reversal is actually "the way things really are." In the native American cultures, different tribes had *contrares*, men who washed with dirt instead of water, or rode their horses backwards. In Lewis Carroll's *Through the Looking Glass*, the White Queen tells Alice, " 'It's a poor sort of memory that only works backwards.' "

Keeping this reversal in mind while reading THE EXPERIMENT will help the reader greatly, because much of what is taught is aimed at getting the student to turn the world upside down and inside out so as to gain a better understanding of ourselves and our place in the Grand Scheme of Things.

When the new ideas come flying at you, and like Alice you cry: " 'I can't believe that,' " remember the sage advice of the White Queen. " 'Can't you?' the Queen said in a pitying tone, 'try again. Draw a long breath and close your eyes.'

"Alice laughed. 'There's no use trying,' she said, 'one can't believe impossible things.'

" 'I daresay you haven't had much practice,' said the Queen. 'When I was your age, I always did it for half an hour a day. Why, sometimes I've believed as many as six impossible things before breakfast.' "

Not many of us have had much practice or encouragement in believing impossible things. Rather, we are instructed to stay on track, keep in line, and not to make waves.

Well, it's time for the waves to roll in, for the world to change, and for new ideas, even impossible ones to come to light. In THE EXPERIMENT, we are constantly encouraged to stretch our minds, to reverse the usual, to accept the unusual, and to consider, at the least, the impossible. This means learning to see and read the basic meaning in the appearances of our daily experience.

The word "Basic," so often mentioned in THE EXPERIMENT, refers to a symbolic language of archetypal energy descriptions that reveals a meaning often hidden beneath the spoken word. In Basic, the root assumption is that the world we see and experience through the outer senses is a reflection, and since reflections always involve some type of reversal, seeing the world through Basic requires that we gradually reverse our habitual way of interpreting daily experience to bring it in line with a larger, more comprehensive viewpoint.

One way of accomplishing this is to find the Basic meaning of the words we use to discover their true intent. The word "consider," for instance, commonly means, "to apply one's mind to something in order to increase one's knowledge or understanding of it or to reach a decision about it; to think about with care or caution." The root of the word "consider" is from the Latin, *Con* - with, and *Sider* - star. The essential meaning of "consider" is "with the stars." In Basic, one increases one's knowledge by aligning "with the stars," to receive information from cosmic sources of wisdom.

The word "desire" is similar. It commonly means, (v.) "to long for or to hope for something," or (n.) "a conscious impulse toward something that promises satisfaction in its attainment." It too has a Latin root, *De* - from, and *Sider* - star: that which comes to us "from the stars." The Basic meaning of "desire" implies that these longings or impulses come to us from the highest sources of energy and power in the universe. This is a reversal of the commonly-held idea that desires can lead one astray or into trouble.

It was interesting to observe that larger essential truths were often found in Sanskrit, Greek and Old English meanings and even in Latin roots, but when the surface meaning of Latin definitions entered the stream of language, a reversal took place. It was obvious that a major shift to mirror viewing had occurred in Roman times. The principal factor in *mirror viewing* is that the attention is turned outward to focus on the world of sensation while largely ignoring the wealth of inner information that is available when one turns within (for instance to align with and receive information "from the stars").

As we were trained to read the Basic meaning beneath the surface appearances, we were put in touch with a common essential definition base, a universal meaning that is aligned with what THE EXPERIMENT calls THE LAW. THE LAW is the Beneficent Force that shapes and structures reality from the other side of the mirror. From this side of the mirror, our reasoning scientific mind says that visible reality is the collection of innumerable specific items, forces, objects, which interact to create the whole. THE LAW says that any given specific originates from the WHOLE, and that the apparent separation between THE WHOLE and each specific manifestation is an illusion, a fact that was evident in our examination of the perception of color and sound.

Our thinking mind, our self-conscious and subconscious levels of awareness, our functions of imaging and discrimination, of defining and identifying. . . these are referred to as our Inner Computer. We can reprogram our inner computers daily, with information bytes based on new interpretations. This is a growing process, and as the new definitions replace the old, we can see the outer reality that surrounds us shifting in accordance with this inner growth.

As we lived in and with THE EXPERIMENT, we gained knowledge and became familiar with the language of Basic. We understood and used the computer-like mechanics in reprogramming our self-conscious definitions and thus our sub-conscious responses to those new definitions. We found an inner set of rules that we could rely on.

The knowledge found in the Silence, in our minds, is the place where each of us can find our own teachers who are always there for us throughout our lives, if we remember to stop - stop the internal dialogue - and listen.

As we enter into the 21st century,
may we achieve a unified consciousness,
that rises above the illusion
of separateness and isolation.

May we, as a unified global society,
enter into the communication
and exchange of ideas with others,
so that all of our interactions reflect
The Law of a Larger and Beneficent Force.

Welcome to THE EXPERIMENT.

K. Michaels & C. Night

PART ONE

<u>MINDBENDING</u>

ON THE VOICES OF THE EXPERIMENT

This book has come into its final form as the result of a unique collaboration. There are several strands weaving through its pages, each one making a contribution from its particular point of view.

First and foremost, of course, is the voice of the teachers. We say teachers, plural, because although there is one teacher who spoke to Ketherin in her weekly sessions, he/she stands at the head of a group of teachers who often added their comments as the teachings progressed. As Ketherin described them, they were often a boisterous lot, fun-loving and humorous, particularly when the subject matter revolved around the foibles of our delicate egos. There was one character she always saw as a tall man, sitting on a wall, and when the group found something the teacher said particularly funny, he was always banging on pots and pans, laughing and making jokes. Ketherin loved her time with the teachers, and always said that it felt like being home.

As she visited with the teachers and wrote down what they said, there were times when she would get visual images and then she would make a quick sketch in the notebook. Corvus would take these and expand them into illustrations, and as the book progressed, he added charts and graphs. While laying out the text of the sessions, he began seeing images to accompany the words and these developed into the illustrations that accompany nearly every page.

Ketherin also wrote a large body of poetry, and her poems, with Corvus's illustrations, are placed at the beginning of each chapter.

At times during the transcription of teaching material there were personal interchanges between Ketherin and the teachers. Sometimes, Ketherin would jot down notes about a dream she had remembered, or an experience she was going through. When relevant, she included them as part of the book. As you can see on the facing page, her comments are set in a different typeface with her initials (K.M.) at the end. The teachers' responses to her are also in a typeface that is different from that of the main body of text. At times the teachers break from dictation to emphasize a point or speak to the reader, and these comments are also set in their distinctive typeface.

The boxed-in areas, such as this one, represent additions to the text. Often Ketherin and Corvus knew that certain material was either assumed or simply left to them to fill in. The exercises, the color experiments, the information on *Triangulation*, minerals and crystals - all these were added as needed while the book was being put together.

This is a multidimensional work and it is our hope that it will awaken in you, the reader, visions of your own multidimensional nature.

INITIAL CONTACT
at
THE CONCEPT POOL

June 2, 1980. Monday

"Relax, child. Let yourself flow with the light. Melt into it. Let all tensions go and feel the light fill you with healing, balancing, cleansing energy. Fill thy whole being with MY light, the One light, the perfect balance and harmony of ALL THAT IS.

You are an extension of ME, a clear and beautiful extension of ALL THAT IS. Today, feel your part in the Whole, feel the perfect working of ALL THAT IS. See its beauty, its perfection, its orderly pattern; and there, see your part in that pattern. ALL THAT IS is your teacher, your life force, your pulse. See all through the light of ALL THAT IS.

As I sat, writing down the teacher's words, I felt that something was about to happen; it made me nervous and a bit edgy. I had been having regular sessions for some time now but something about today was different - I just didn't know what. My teacher reassured me. . . KM.

Today is a day to stay centered, calm and secure in your place of Inner Stillness and light. Keep the pace even, the view positive, the actions joyful. Walk in Beauty. See the lovely edge to all things, the funny edge, the true edge.

I shall switch you to a higher level of reception now.
Stay centered and relaxed.

It was at this moment (mentioned in the Preface) that I felt myself almost catapulted into a space so vast, so grand that it made my breath catch in my throat. Towering Beings with deep, resonant voices that echoed in my head greeted me and began to speak. . . KM.

You are a receiver, an instrument built and tuned to receive. Tune yourself into a greater plane, a larger and faster plane of vibration and listen to these WORDS, these sound structures.

In the open, receptive area of this larger plane you have available to you a pool of concepts, like a gene pool. These IDEAS float freely, with a life of their own, available to those who are magnetically constructed on similar WAVE LENGTHS, of similar sound structures.

As you swim through this reservoir of ideas, concepts or thoughts, you may pick and choose at will the grouped, packaged thought units, and transfer them, through your language definitions, your inner computer tapes, into defined and shaped sounds or ideas.

Your reality is one specific, directed, confined focus, set on all sides by and only by the limits of definition. Swim in this multidimensional pool of sound combinations, energy constructs and choose those which can translate into your time-space zone or focus.

We are all multi-constructs, experiencing in multi-awareness levels to add to the One-ness of ALL THAT IS, through multi-Oneness. We are each ALL THAT IS. There are no real unit definitions that separate us. We are multifaceted energy constructs, all of One, interacting, affecting all, as all.

The seeming separation between you and ALL THAT IS is slight illusion. Your reality is ready now to expand into a new focus. Great segments of energy shall totally shift in the coming changes which, on your plane, may appear as land upheavals, death and destruction: all forms of change.

This shift shall also appear as the NEW, which it becomes. A mountain that stretches and shifts on the skin of your earth, a physical earth change, is an energy transfer. A tree that falls beneath molten lava shall shift its focus and, therefore, its appearance, and perhaps become an animal of the New Age, or one of a myriad of multidimensional choices in line magnetically with its prediliction.

Perhaps a tree that lived without human contact on a mountain near the timber line shall choose this time to join its previous treeness with a human structure and, as a part of a human mold, incorporate into that human a love and appreciation of isolated mountains, of the nobility and importance of tree life on earth. Do you love the water, and is part of your love of it TREE MEMORY, of rain falling and roots drinking, of air filled with water which you thirstily drank, AS A TREE?

It may be you of whom we speak, and not only the YOU who reads this but the multi-you, the faceted you which interconnects with all you's; ALL THAT IS.

We are all all things. We who SPEAK to you have experienced your channel, your focus, your time-space zone of shaped, defined and constructed reality. It is a rich and intense experience and part of a Great Experiment.

Directed sound, directed realities ... these are our 'control' experiments where consciousness, a basic of ALL THAT IS, is gently shaped and molded by sound into free-flowing, spontaneous end results.

We aim at expansion, beauty, order and harmony. We play, with love, at the making of worlds, the guiding of energy. We soak your reality in shaped energy. The closest word to describe this energy is LOVE.

We beam this LOVE into your time-space zone as colored sound, harmonized into mathematical combinations, destined to achieve order and beauty. It will be a spontaneous result but it will, as planned, of necessity, be harmonious and beautiful, a physical expression of LOVE.

Earth has long been in preparation for the reception of these concepts: accurate definitions of life, of how realities work, and how each of you, as conscious, active participants may help to shape your perception and experiences.

Through the well-directed, joyfully-chosen beams of LOVE for all on earth, you shall create a New earth, a new world, where all is beauty: loved for its ingenuity of construction, its joy and humor of expression. These are all ideas, directions your reality is taking, and if it seems ahead of its time, be patient. Look within and see that this new world already exists.

Keep your receptors stretched. Do not seek the GLUE of your everyday world, but get used to the heights, the thin air. Swim in this concept pool often. Bring down, translate into your own language the workings of the Law you see here and share it with others. Keep your awareness of our largeness with you at a conscious level.

Return to ALL THAT IS. Join us often, and build in yourself the open pool of Love and Light which we ALL are."

High amid the mountains blue
Sparkling peaks of changing hue
Granite walls form the crown
Opaline, circle the town

Of No-name.

Lapis blue reflects the sun
Rivulets down the mighty walls run
Meet in song in the valley's bed
Greeting us as we are led

To No-name.

Enter now
Feel the sweet breeze on your cheek.

Stone paths spiral through the town
Yellow roofs a golden crown
Trees and beast, bird and man
Flourish in this wondrous land

Of No-name.

Time is one and there is none
All is ended, all begun
Thought with humor fair and mild
Earth's sweet nature loves its child

In No-name.

Smell the fragrant olibanum.

All remembered, naught is lost
Spring is one with dew and frost
Star is one with moon and sun
Now our tale it has begun

In No-name.

CHART OF THE KEY OF E-MAJOR

CHAPTER ONE
STARTING WITH EVERYTHING

Friday, June 6, 1980.

I'm thrilled at starting THE EXPERIMENT, *a book that I have known, all my life, that I would write, but I also find myself wondering why the teachers seem to be writing about what has already been said so well by others. . . KM.*

"Relax, child, into the light. You ask why receive all this information when others translate it so well, like Seth (a reference to the Seth books written by Jane Roberts and Robert Butts)? Seth paints grand landscapes of design, describing your and neighboring realities, focuses, but we shall deal directly with SHAPED SOUND, DIRECTED ENERGY. This is a focus of the instruction in THE EXPERIMENT, and an important unit to be added to the knowledge of the whole.

"We shall use the charts, the metered, measured vibrations of sound and color, to achieve specific results. The charts are a brief but important beginning in the practical work of directing energy."

This first stroll around the concept pool may feel like the teachers are holding your head under the surface of the concept pool for rather too long, but perhaps that is the nature of starting with everything, rather than starting with one thing and working up to everything. And that, of course, is the first lesson.

Chapter One is the crucible in which our brains are melted down prior to being recast in the mold that will allow us a clearer glimpse of what it means to live in a mirror reflective reality. If you find it confusing, remember that the teachers are speaking from the other side of the mirror, trying to get us to see things from their perspective. Until a basis for understanding is developed and laid in place, you may naturally feel somewhat disconnected. Persevere! Read it through a few times as the teachers recommend. Once you make it through Chapter One, you will be ready for anything.

SOME NOTES ON THE CORRELATION OF SOUND AND COLOR

The diatonic or Major scale is the familiar *do re mi* (diagram at right) a scale which traverses an octave of sound in seven steps and returns on the eighth note to the original tone. This original

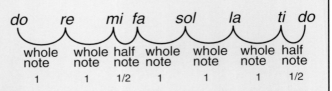

tone (do) can be any note whatsoever (C, D, E, etc.); it is the structure of the scale that remains the same, half steps between the third and fourth, seventh and eighth notes, whole steps between the other notes. This particular structure emphasizes the relationships of harmony within an octave of sound, whatever the key.

On the other hand, if all the spaces between the whole steps in the diatonic scale were filled in with half tones (semitones), the result would be an equally divided octave of twelve semitones, a neutral scale which emphasizes no particular harmonic relationships. Then, instead of the diatonic or major scale, the resulting scale is called the chromatic scale of music.

THE CHROMATIC SCALE OF MUSIC
Twelve equally-spaced semitones rising in pitch, spanning an octave of sound vibration, so that the thirteenth tone is the same as the first, only doubled in frequency, higher in pitch. The shaded notes represent the diatonic scale of C-Major in relationship to the chromatic scale.

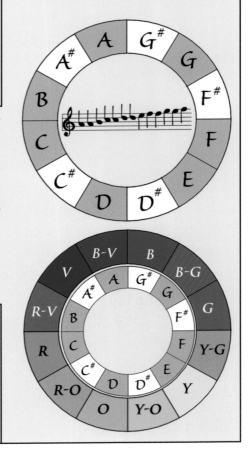

This is similar to the chromatic scale of color, which divides an octave of light, the solar spectrum, into twelve equally-spaced colors. The two scales invite comparison and there are many systems which correlate the twelve musical tones of the chromatic scale of music with the twelve chromatic colors. In the system of correlation used in THE EXPERIMENT, the note of C is the sound frequency that corresponds to the light frequency of red.

THE CHROMATIC SCALE OF COLOR
Twelve equally-spaced colors, beginning with the wavelength of red light and rising in frequency through the entire series, ending with red-violet. There is only one octave of visible light (the solar spectrum) which starts with red and ends with violet. The inclusion of red-violet as the twelfth chromatic color links the first color, red, with the last color, violet, to complete the circle.

THE CHARTS

Even before the opening session that started THE EXPERIMENT, earlier sessions had instructed us to begin work on a painting, the first music chart, based on the note of E.

So, what does music look like? How would you make a painting of the note of E natural?

Let's see...we could look, first, at the notes in the Key of E, see what their colors are and go from there.
E would be Yellow.
Up a third would be G-sharp, Blue.
Up a fifth would be B-natural, Red-violet.
OK...let's start with the note of E, colored yellow.

We began making preliminary sketches. It was clear that the starting point was to be the note of E natural, and earlier studies had pointed out a correlation between musical notes and colors (see facing page), so we knew that E natural could be represented by the color yellow. The next step was to surround the yellow note of E with the notes/colors found in the key of E Major (the *do re mi . . .* scale structure, p. 24 & facing page). When *do* is yellow, then *re* is green, *mi* is blue, and so on through the scale (see the colorbar).

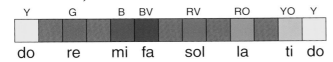

Y	G	B	BV	RV	RO	YO	Y
do	re	mi	fa	sol	la	ti	do

There is also a spatial relationship between the notes of the Major scale: the progression of *do re mi* requires half steps between some notes and whole steps between others. This structure of half and whole notes is what gives the chart its basic shape.

Over the next week or two, we prepared a large (4' x 4') piece of masonite by putting on the white background and laying out the grid that would be the matrix for the chart. A lot of our preparation time was spent in mixing paints to get just the right hues of color. The color experiments in contrast from the Point of View turned out to be the perfect tool for fine-tuning our hues. We would lay out pairs of opposite color cards and gaze at one of the colors under north light, comparing its afterimage against the other color card and making adjustments. The trick was to get the afterimage from one color card to be the same hue as the card representing the opposite color. By tuning each pair of opposites in this way we arrived at a balanced palette of twelve colors (see facing page). We then painted after work and on weekends, and soon the chart was finished (see p. 38).

We are laying out the process we went through in creating the chart because the teachers used the way we approached it to begin their lessons on reversal and the effects of living in a mirror reflective reality.

"Notice," they said, "that in the sequence you followed, the yellow note of E is the starting point which you developed into the chart you are doing of the Key of E. Now, when the yellow is surrounded, on earth, in your reality, with complementary note and color combinations, it becomes enhanced, enlarged and strengthened. The accompanying notes and colors keep the yellow note of E on track, in line, much like a dog herding sheep. As any musician knows, the notes in the Key of E Major align and enhance the sound of the note of E. They define the sound of the note of E.

The reversal, which you may not see, is that in actuality, the chart makes the note of E rather than the note of E making the chart, which, when seen from your reality's focus, it seems to do, and does. But accuracy demands a reversal and the knowledge that the chart creates the sound of the note of E.

So, what may we deduce here? That by surrounding the note of E with the chart, the sound of the note of E is

Made, constructed, sounded,
Strengthened, enlarged, and
<u>DIRECTED</u>!

This is a much larger concept than you realize! It is one that will make the concept mind stretch to understand it. As we proceed, you will begin to see the usefulness of this and how it may be worked in your reality.

The surrounding note and color combinations
act to keep the sound, the color, on track, in line.

From the side of the mirror where you stand, earth perception, the surrounding notes and colors appear to develop from your choice of the note of E as the starting point, but, in actuality, it is the Chart with the surrounding notes and colors that creates the sound of the note of E.

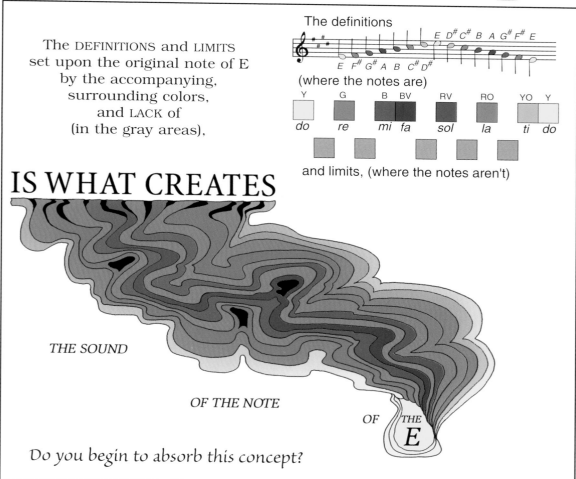

The DEFINITIONS and LIMITS
set upon the original note of E
by the accompanying,
surrounding colors,
and LACK of
(in the gray areas),

The definitions

(where the notes are)

do   re   mi   fa   sol   la   ti   do

and limits, (where the notes aren't)

IS WHAT CREATES

THE SOUND

OF THE NOTE

OF THE E

Do you begin to absorb this concept?

In the major scale of music, the positions of the notes are determined by the "intervals," the spaces between the notes, the sounds of silence. In the chart of the Key of E Major, these in between spaces are filled with gray. The interaction between the colors of the Key of E and the gray areas, between the visible and *invisible* aspects of the chart, produces an energy surge because each side of the chart gives an energy boost to the other.

This leads us into the area of two important anomalies.

ANOMALY: a deviation from the norm; an irregularity; anything abnormal

43

The first anomaly involves the *interaction* between the gray areas and the colored areas that creates the *energy-producing effect* of the chart. The gray areas in the E Major chart are influenced by the surrounding colors and are filled in automatically by the eye with violets and yellows - mostly violets - according to the laws of contrast. In the predominantly yellow color chart, the human eye reads the neutral gray as violet. (The gray is influenced the most by yellow, since yellow is the main color-tone in the chart. This is similar to the way a musical key imparts a distinct mood tone to a composition written in that key.)

Wait a minute. The eye reads gray as violet? That makes no sense at all.

Here, try the color experiment. It may not "make sense" but it works.

COLOR EXPERIMENT

Stare fixedly at the yellow square under a bright light for thirty seconds, then shift your gaze to the blank area. Try this before reading the explanation.

The afterimage is always the complementary opposite of the color being viewed, so the yellow background changes to its opposite, violet (see the Point of View, LIGHT AND COLOR, for an explanation of opposites). The opposite of gray is gray so the expected afterimage of the inner square would be gray, but the eye reads the gray square as violet, and produces the complementary opposite of violet which is yellow.

Due to the action of Simultaneous Contrast, the dominant color, yellow, influences the gray square to take on a violet color cast. Then, the action of Successive Contrast causes the violet/gray square to produce the yellow afterimage.

I got it! Since the inner square on the bottom turns yellow, that proves that the eye is reading the gray square as violet. OK. So what's next? How does this produce energy?

These gray/violet areas in the chart charge the yellow construct, the yellow tone of the chart. The eye also edges the gray/violet squares with yellow, to achieve a balance, a full circle of violet to yellow to violet. (If you gaze at the gray square, the yellow highlights around the edges appear almost immediately.) This yellow edging is a more intense hue than the yellow square and further enhances the violet, charging it with greater energy which in turn charges the yellow.

So as you look at the chart, the interplay between the colored (visible) and gray (invisible) aspects begins to build up a flow of energy.

This may seem abstract to you but the energy transformations at work in the color charts have a deep if somewhat hidden connection with your moment-to-moment existence.

I can really "see" the energy interplay going on in the chart. As I look at the yellow highlights around the gray square, I feel an energy surge, but what, exactly, is this doing? How does this affect me?

The chart illustrates how your energy becomes transformed and enhanced by the interplay between the visible and invisible aspects of reality. Earth existence is a world of duality. On the one hand is everything you see, everything you think, say and do. On the other hand is a vast but invisible field from which thoughts, events and circumstances seem to arise.

The body has conscious functions that are under your direct control, but it also has functions that are carried out invisibly, seemingly beyond your control. By way of illustration, consider the following analogy. You plant a seed in the ground - a conscious act. The earth receives the seed and in a mysterious and invisible process, the form within the seed is stimulated to grow and take shape.

In a similar fashion, the invisible arena that surrounds you, like the gray area in the color chart, or the earth receiving the seed, receives the impression of your every thought, word and deed. Everything that you think, say or do shapes the energy coming through you, and this sculpted energy is impressed into the invisible but highly reflective medium that surrounds you. The same process that enhances the yellow or that causes the seed to grow, charges your thoughts, words and deeds, amplifies and extends them, and reflects them back to you as event and circumstance. This is the essence of how each of you creates your own reality, moment by moment, thought by thought, step by step.

Your reactions to this effect and your subsequent choices re-charge the invisible side and continue the process, the interaction, and over a period of time, this interplay between conscious and subconscious activity builds up a flow of energy that determines the shape, the tone and the details of your life experience. That experience can be positive or negative, fulfilling or destructive, depending upon the choices you make, but, either way, the primary effect of the interaction between visible and invisible is movement. Like the constantly-shifting magnetic pulses that turn a magnetically-powered turntable (Dark Ages analogy), or that power a particle accelerator, the yellow-violet-gray poles in the chart fluctuate, switch back and forth. . .

TO CREATE MOVEMENT!

THAT IS WHY OPPOSITES EXIST -
TO CREATE MOVEMENT.

AHA!
Anomaly number one, right?
I've got it! . . . I think.

OK. Let's look at another anomaly: the idea that
THE CHART CREATES THE SOUND OF THE NOTE OF E.

As the interplay between the colors and the gray areas builds up movement, the chart "gets up to speed" and its energy produces a vibration which actually sounds the note of E on the invisible side, at a level inaudible to the human ear. This is similar to the way a vibration that rises above a certain pitch leaves the range of human hearing and becomes inaudible. It vibrates, but on the invisible side; it is not perceived by the physical senses.

Although it appears that the sound of the note of E, the color yellow,
is the origin of the chart,
the mirror-reflection is that
the chart with all the note and color combinations
creates the sound of the note of E.

From the earth point of view, the sound of the note of E is the starting point that leads to the chart, but at the same time, the chart with all the surrounding note and color combinations creates the sound of the note of E.

So which is it? Does the chart create the sound of the note of E, or is the note of E the origin of the chart? Since earth reality is reflective, both processes are happening at once. One is the *reflection*, the appearance, and the other is the *Reflector*, That which Reflects. Hold a small mirror up to the illustration below and read the diagram in both directions. The E creates the Key creates the Chart creates the Key creates the E.

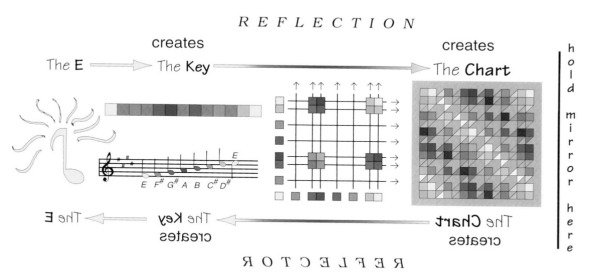

The only thing that makes one situation seem normal and the other one anomalous is the illusion that time flows in only one direction. Scientists know that at the subatomic level time is not a limit. Some form of instantaneous "knowing" connects all the subatomic particles in the Universe, and influences reach forward and backward in time. So consider for a moment that time is a feature of the *reflection*, hence reversed in appearance. From this viewpoint (the *Reflector* view) an event or an experience exists in its complete form and unfolds backwards in time. To the perception caught in the isolated channel of the illusion of time (the *reflection)*, events appear to unfold forward, piece by piece, into completion. (The *Reflector* view is practiced in traditions where the student of creative visualization is taught to see the desired reality in detail, complete and whole, not "in the future," but in the present moment. This aligns the student with the SOURCE of the desire, the WHOLE, and acts to collapse, or shorten, the intervening period of time and space between the desire and its fulfilment.)

The earth appearance is that the sound of the note of E, the color yellow, is the origin of the chart of E Major, but accuracy demands a reversal of the appearance and an acceptance of the knowledge that it is the whole chart with the surrounding notes and colors that creates the sound of the single note of E.

Compare this with the color experiment in Light and Color where the sight of the single color (the *reflection*) leads the perception to an awareness of the whole spectrum of color, while (from the *Reflector*) the whole spectrum is the origin of the specific color.

an example from acoustics - the way we hear the sound of a vibrating string. The earth, space-time appearance is that when the string of an instrument is plucked, we hear the vibration as a single, isolated tone. Yet we know from the study of acoustics that the plucked string simultaneously vibrates in a whole range of modes, producing a series of notes (called the harmonic series, or overtones) that the ear doesn't distinguish or separate from the (apparently) single note that we perceive as the fundamental tone.

Although the soundwaves corresponding to the harmonic overtones all strike the eardrum, only the fundamental tone, the wavelength corresponding to the vibration of the full length of the string, is consciously heard. The entire harmonic series created by the plucked string exists on the invisible side, unnoticed; yet because of the way the harmonics influence what we hear as the fundamental, it is the combination of all these accompanying, surrounding inaudible notes which creates the sound we hear as the fundamental tone.

*All the notes in the experience combine
to produce the perception of a single, separate tone.*

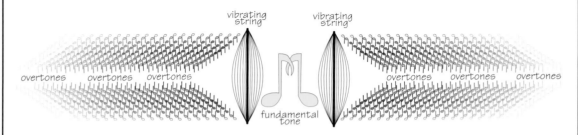

The infinite waves of sound create the experience of the single tone, the fundamental, which creates the infinite waves of harmonic overtones.

This is an important point: that directed, shaped energy (the earth experience) is created, in isolated, specific channels, by the seeming effect it creates.

Relate this once more to the color experiment: the sight of red is the shaped energy, the earth experience, and the effect of looking at red (or any color) is to then become aware of the whole spectrum of color. But we have already demonstrated that the whole spectrum is the origin of the specific color. Thus we can say that directed, shaped energy, the color red, is created in an isolated, specific channel (the eye/brain connection) by the seeming effect it creates: all color.

In other words,
THE EFFECT CREATES THE ORIGINAL.
The chart creates the sound of the note of E,

You think that it is the other way around
because of the way it appears to you on your reflective reality,

MIRROR IMAGED
MIRROR IMAGED

You see this reversal at work in all the laws of sight and perception in your reality.

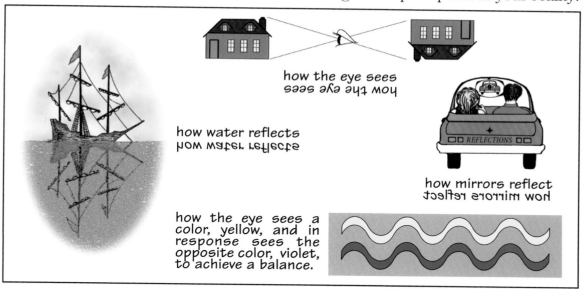

how the eye sees
how the eye sees

how water reflects
how water reflects

how mirrors reflect
how mirrors reflect

how the eye sees a color, yellow, and in response sees the opposite color, violet, to achieve a balance.

This (the opposites) is what creates movement, or rather,
Movement creates the illusion of opposites!

Try to absorb this. Make this a working and total part of your definition of reality. The chart creates the E. Movement creates the appearance of opposites.

Is this a version of anomaly number one, about opposites creating movement? It's a mirror reflection, right?

That's right, and it all has to do with the cosmic Law of Motion.

It's well-known that differences create movement (this is the principle that makes a thermostat work) and that opposites create the most movement (cold, dry air meeting warm, wet air makes the movement of a thunderstorm).

From your point of view in three-dimensional space-time (the *reflection*), opposite effects appear and interact, creating movement. From the other side of the mirror, (the *Reflector*), the Law of Motion predominates:

Motion creates the *appearance of opposites.*

Remember that the first emanation from the MONAD is a movement from unity to duality. This primal movement creates the opposite poles and makes vibration possible (Point of View, Sound and Music). From the earth perspective you experience the opposites and tend to forget the unity from which they arise.

When the eye sees yellow, it creates violet.
More accurately, the violet is in the yellow, or
yellow is one way of seeing the energy current
called yellow and appearing as yellow
but, in actuality, yellowviolet,

a line of directed, shaped, defined, limited, sound, color vibration
which your body knows and sees in its fullness: yellow/violet.

Your incorrect definitions say "only yellow," but there is no such thing as only yellow. Yellow is always also violet. There is no real separation. There can not be one. The separation is an illusion. The eye knows better and the body knows. Only the defining tape need be changed, and the body, working with the Law, shall accomplish the rest.

Keep in mind that on earth, the Law of Polarity (see Glossary) is in operation, and the pendulum swings from pole to pole.

When yellow is correctly defined as yellow-violet, or better yet, as yellow-violet-yellow-violet-yellow-violet, this allows a smooth flow from one pole to its opposite and back. The mind experiences a completed circuit, and the result is stabilization. But if the mind, with its learned definitions, tries to force an incorrect assumption of one color only, then there is a bounce-back reaction, a magnetic repulsion that propels the pendulum to the opposite pole with a force equal to that used in holding the single color (or idea) on a single, off-center point.

Color Experiment

Try holding the gaze motionless on the yellow square under a bright light for more than a few seconds. The eye experiences the magnetic repulsion of "one color only" as the violet highlights begin to jump and twitch on the edge of the yellow square.

THERE IS NO SUCH THING AS "ONLY YELLOW."

It is

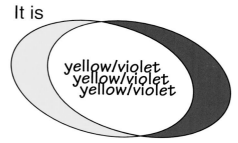

yellow/violet
yellow/violet
yellow/violet

FIG 1. WHEN THE EYE SEES YELLOW, IT AUTOMATICALLY BRINGS TOGETHER

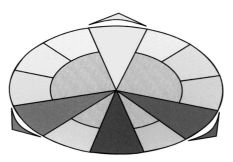

RED AND BLUE TO MAKE VIOLET, THUS EXPERIENCING THE ENTIRE SPECTRUM.

and as the eye swings from yellow to violet to yellow, the whole cycle of colors is experienced since complementary colors complete the spectrum. (See FIG. 1).

This supports two ideas.

First, as the eye passes from yellow to violet and back to yellow there develops a rhythm, a circular motion which encompasses the full spectrum of color. Since each color is charged by its opposite there is also an energy surge between one occurrence of yellow and the next, leading the circular motion into a spiral.

> THUS THE SHAPE OF DIRECTED ENERGY,
> THE SPIRAL OF MANIFESTATION,
> IS DEFINED.

Second, since the sight of one specific color automatically creates the whole spectrum, and since your reality is a mirror reflection of the LAW at work, then it follows that the WHOLE (spectrum) creates the SPECIFIC (color).

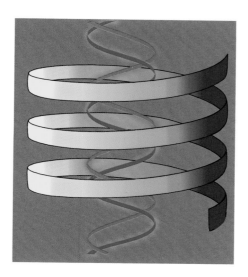

Work on this reversal of definition. See the LAW at work: the creation of the SINGLE by the WHOLE, the creation of the sound of the note of E by the chart.

See this reversal at work in the appearance of a blue shirt. The shirt absorbs ALL colors EXCEPT blue, ie. yellow and red, and therefore creates the _appearance_ of blue.

Now, you are just beginning to absorb this concept from the pool of energy you are "swimming" in.

white light source

AHA! Blue shirt

> IN YOUR REALITY,
> TO CREATE SOMETHING
> TAKES ALL THE REST,
> ITS OPPOSITE, AND THEN,
> IN YOUR MIRRORED FOCUS,
> IT APPEARS.

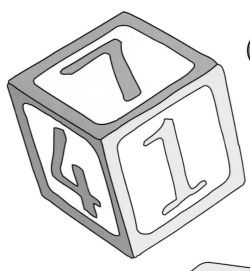

There is no *one*
without all other numbers.

All other numbers create *one*,
and yet to you, it appears that
all numbers are created *by one*.

Since each larger unit
can be broken down to
a *one* unit
you conclude that
the *one* unit
is the origin.

Origin and specific.

These two terms
are interchangeable
in your reality.

To be accurate, the origin is
THE ALL, ALL THAT IS, THE WHOLE.

IT creates the specific,
the *one*, the unit,
in the same way that blue only
appears when all other colors
unite, combine.

The separation, to make a unit appear is only possible from the WHOLE.
Blue only appears when all other colors except blue unite, combine.

← COLORS WITHOUT ANY BLUE → ← COLORS CONTAINING BLUE →

COLOR EXPERIMENT: Cover all the color strips on the page except for the one just below. Then, under a bright light, scan your eyes slowly back and forth over the strip from red to yellow. Do this for a while, back and forth, until you feel the afterimage building up. Then look at a blank space or close your eyes.
WHEN ALL OTHER COLORS EXCEPT BLUE UNITE AND COMBINE, THEN BLUE APPEARS.

This has great mathematical possibilities, as can be seen when approached from that which reflects on the mirror rather than by reading the mirror itself.

You know how hard it is
to read a book in the mirror.
So it is by reading appearances
in your earth reality.

KNOW:
THAT THE WHOLE (SPECTRUM) CREATES THE SINGLE (COLOR).
A SINGLE ALWAYS APPEARS DOUBLE (THE COLOR AND ITS OPPOSITE).
OPPOSITES CREATE MOVEMENT, OR,
MOVEMENT CREATES THE APPEARANCE OF OPPOSITES

Again: the whole makes the unit.
The unit appears separate by a combination of elements
chosen to create the seeming single unit
in the same way blue appears by combining all but blue.

The appearance of blue automatically creates
THAT WHICH IT IS - orange, and is what it originally was and is:
ALL COLORS, ALL THAT IS

There is more, but that is enough for now. Read and re-read this until you fully understand it. Absorb it into your definitions. We shall continue.
Welcome to our energy pool. Share with others what you learn here. Make it a full part of your being.

AT ANGLES, AT EVERY DEGREE

A world of yellow orange sand
  With an indigo sky hung low
    I mount Capella's crimson back
      And off through the desert we go.

    As the wind we travel across the globe
      Picking up speed, so that I
        Can see what was once invisible
          To my very slow naked eye.

      Faster and faster we travel,
        Lights flashing so brightly past me
          When suddenly all that was moving
            Seems to have stopped, and I see

        Lines reaching in every direction
          Great pulsating tubes filled with lights
        A grid of climbable ladders,
      Reaching through infinite heights.

Off to my left, off to my right,
At angles, at every degree,
Above me, below me, wherever I look
The ladders of light beckon me.

I slide off her back, her coat of soft silk
She smiles with her eyes of the night
And nudges me gently
With her warm nose
As I quickly climb out of sight.

Moments or years have passed, and I'm back.
I tell her of all that I've seen.
Worlds filled with wonder, different and strange
Now it all seems as a dream.

The colors, the smells, the sounds and forms,
The Beauty of all I behold
Is wider and greater and finer and brighter
Than ever as yet has been told.

June 9, 1980. Monday

It's one week now since the teachers began the book. I'm sitting at my desk waiting for them to come through, making some notes and playing with a multifaceted cut glass crystal on the desk. As I look through the crystal, I see my normal view faceted and curved like a view through a kaleidescope. I'm feeling restless, not having slept well, and having trouble keeping a positive view firm. When the teachers begin, they reassure me. KM

"Relax child, into the Light. You are having a reaction to our sessions - you are feeling less than prime because you are meeting resistances to the large amounts of energy coming through you. There is no need to resist - that is based on old misinterpretations of the danger of so much power. Trace down and eliminate any fragments of those old misconceptions and free yourself to continue our meetings at the concept pool. No harm can come to you. You are protected in the One Light, ever constant, ever healing. Only your mind's doubts or fears can bring minor bodily discomforts.

"So, bask in the One Light. Fill your being with healing balancing light. We have been preparing you since childhood for just this. Have confidence that we know our job and do it well - as you will do. Rest assured in Us, child, for we are you, we are One, united to bring forth this information as a team of friends, brothers. We are of one family, one unit, dedicated to teaching, to spreading Light, Love, the Word. This experience reaches far into other realities - a multidimensional experience. Have faith that it works! It does. We work it. You, as an extension of Us and We, as an extension of you - there really is no separation between us.

"Don't doubt that you can keep these sessions up, because we keep them going. You really cannot close them off - they are happening all the time."

CHAPTER TWO
THE SHAPE OF REALITY

When you hold a multifaceted crystal to your eye, you begin to glimpse a truer, more accurate vision of reality.

The single view that you normally see with two eyes is fractured by the facets of the crystal into a pattern of overlapping aspects, each one containing a piece of the larger view.

Your (earth) focus is like *one* of those aspects, a fragmented, only seemingly-separate unit, similar to a spoke on a wheel. The spoke may have its existence as one of the separate parts that make up the wheel, but from a larger perspective, it is an aspect of the whole, interconnected and integrated into the function of the wheel.

As you can see in the view through the crystal, there is no end, no beginning, no separation between the aspects of the whole.

Each reality is like that: a mathematical focus, a combination of elements, spontaneously interrelating, constantly changing, moving on arcs of mathematical proportion, curves on the spiral of manifestation.

The way that your earth perception takes an angle, or an aspect of the curve on the spiral, and makes it into the one and only reality, is a distortion, an *angle distortion.*

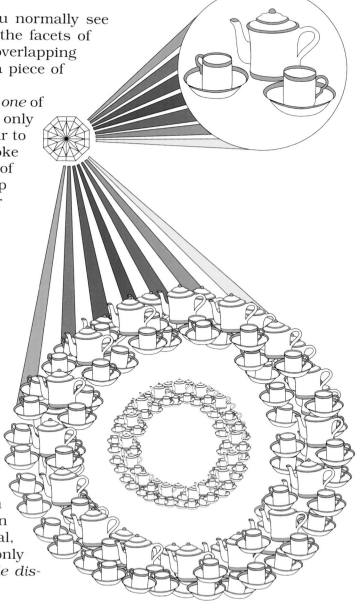

Like the hub of a wheel, each reality radiates out Spokes, variations of itself, in all directions. Since every reality does this, then each reality or focus acts as a center point. If we apply the LAW that each individual focus, each center point, is a reflection of a larger and more encompassing energy structure, then we must conclude the obvious: that the true centerpoint, the original centerpoint,

is THE ALL.

We then see that all variations are mirror reflections of
ALL THAT IS.

(As I'm writing this, I see an image of a billion spokes, all blending with their neighbors and then the view begins to zoom out, farther and farther, until I see this giant energy ball containing ALL these revolving spokes, a huge focus point of spokes, or, as the teachers call it, a Spoke-Focus. . . KM.)

Each facet of focus is an offshoot, a Spoke, revolving, reacting and interacting with itself.

Each focus is unique because of its place on the curve, its mathematical proportion.

If you stay within the confined limits of three-dimensional materialization, the laws of this focus apply and everything on earth seems to prove its working.

From atoms to planets in orbit, *appearances* are there to show you the *definitions* of your reality's *limits*, but since you cannot isolate or separate any one focus (just as there is no 'only yellow'), then the
LIMITS ARE AN ILLUSION.

First we must work within the *appearance* of limits for you to be able to go beyond them with your awareness. Our goal is for all that we teach to be accomplished with the conscious mind. In the New Age this faculty of the human mind shall become manifest and your awareness will extend itself to a new level.

❖   ❖   ❖

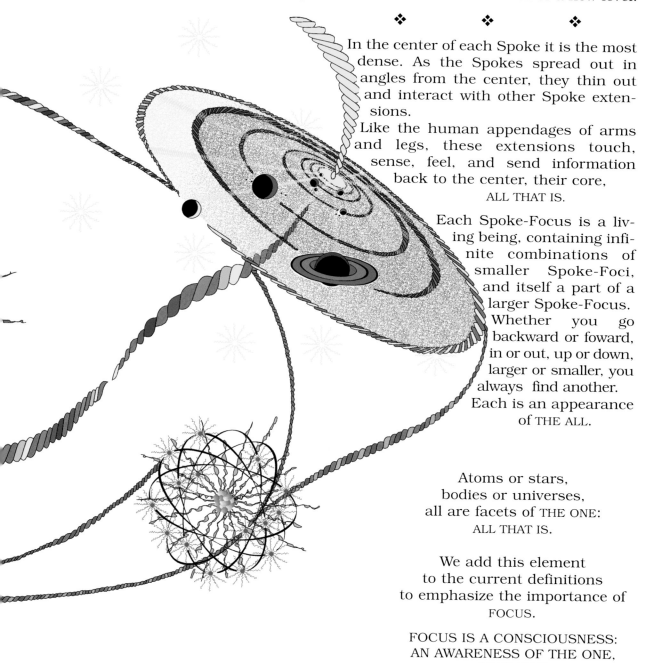

In the center of each Spoke it is the most dense. As the Spokes spread out in angles from the center, they thin out and interact with other Spoke extensions.

Like the human appendages of arms and legs, these extensions touch, sense, feel, and send information back to the center, their core, ALL THAT IS.

Each Spoke-Focus is a living being, containing infinite combinations of smaller Spoke-Foci, and itself a part of a larger Spoke-Focus. Whether you go backward or foward, in or out, up or down, larger or smaller, you always find another. Each is an appearance of THE ALL.

Atoms or stars,
bodies or universes,
all are facets of THE ONE:
ALL THAT IS.

We add this element
to the current definitions
to emphasize the importance of
FOCUS.

FOCUS IS A CONSCIOUSNESS:
AN AWARENESS OF THE ONE,
AS ITSELF,
IN INFINITE FORM.

59

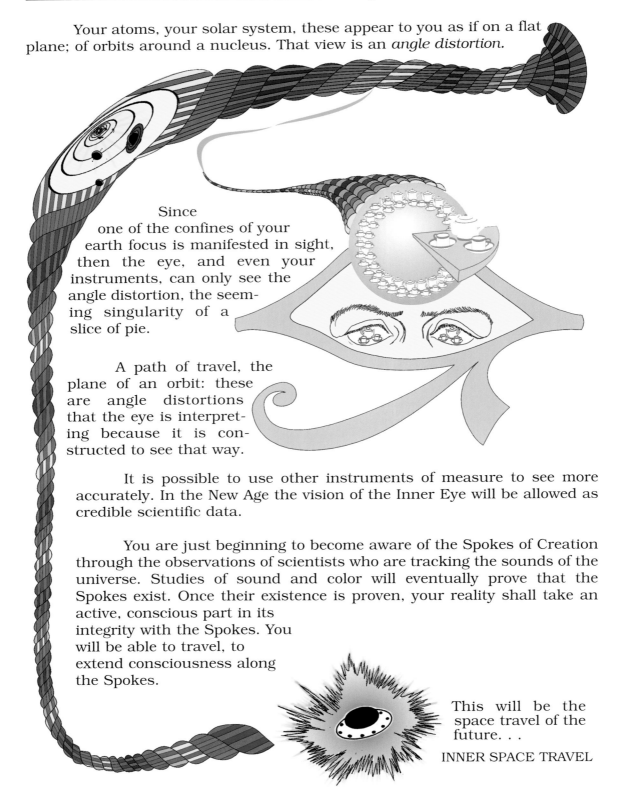

Your atoms, your solar system, these appear to you as if on a flat plane; of orbits around a nucleus. That view is an _angle distortion._

Since one of the confines of your earth focus is manifested in sight, then the eye, and even your instruments, can only see the angle distortion, the seeming singularity of a slice of pie.

A path of travel, the plane of an orbit: these are angle distortions that the eye is interpreting because it is constructed to see that way.

It is possible to use other instruments of measure to see more accurately. In the New Age the vision of the Inner Eye will be allowed as credible scientific data.

You are just beginning to become aware of the Spokes of Creation through the observations of scientists who are tracking the sounds of the universe. Studies of sound and color will eventually prove that the Spokes exist. Once their existence is proven, your reality shall take an active, conscious part in its integrity with the Spokes. You will be able to travel, to extend consciousness along the Spokes.

This will be the space travel of the future. . .

INNER SPACE TRAVEL

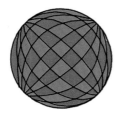
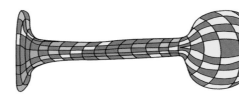

SPHERICAL IS THE SECRET.

GET BEYOND THE ILLUSIONS
OF FLAT PLANE INTERPRETATION.

<u>Scientists</u>: do not rely on what the eye gives as evidence. Go beyond these limits. Use sound, space displacement, and refracted color measures.

Track the shapes of heat and light in space; track any isolated vibration and make maps of the invisible by charting the effects of what you cannot see.

Heat shadows of stars tell you not only what the star does, but also of that which is invisible, of that which surrounds the star.

This note to scientists was very deliberate. As I was writing down their words, the teachers seemed to break from normal dictation for a moment and direct their focus toward those women and men who are exploring the cosmos, in hopes of leading them beyond, or through the illusion. . . KM.

Here we may tie in a music chart.
The E Major chart is like a star,
a universe, a Spoke-Focus.

FOUR MUSIC CHARTS COMBINED

The yellow square that represents the note of E
seems to radiate out and make the chart,
but if the chart makes the sound of the note of E,
then the Spokes make the Focus,
the myriad make the ONE,
the many make the few.

Your (earth-centered) assumption is that the focus is the origin and that
 nter point radiates out a series of variables.

 is correct (from an earth-centered per-
 ive), but since reality is not linear, not
 laned, that perception is an illu-
 Moreover, the time sequence
 se to see the creation of
 enter first and then
 pokes is inaccurate.
 the center and the
 exist at once, *simul-*
 usly.

 want to chart origin
 not time sequence),
 hen the Spoke
 origin of the Focus.

 You may see your
 pt mind stretching
 reversing concepts,
 gning them magneti-
 o the poles of the LAW of
 NE. This correct magnetic
 nent will open the flood gates,
 ing a safe and steady flow of energy to
 through you, rather than the reversed
 etic, repulsing energy of incorrect defini-

 n a magnet is lined up with the earth's
 netic field (north-seeking pole pointing
 h), the two energy fields join. Their lines
 rce unite and the energy of the earth's
 netic field flows through the smaller
 net's field (FIG. A).

 n a magnet's North pole is pointing
 th, the individual magnetic field repuls-
 the earth's lines of force. It separates
 lf and becomes isolated (FIG. B).

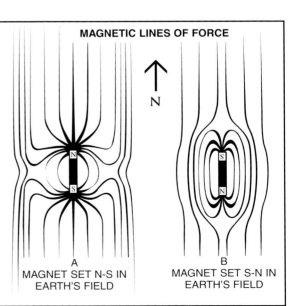

MAGNETIC LINES OF FORCE

N

A
MAGNET SET N-S IN
EARTH'S FIELD

B
MAGNET SET S-N IN
EARTH'S FIELD

These are simple, basic concepts.

The Spoke creates the Focus,
the chart creates the sound of the note of E,
the ALL creates the ONE, the specific.

Remember to look behind the appearance
to see what reflects onto the mirror.
If something appears on the mirror (the earth stage)
that is your evidence that it is reversed.

READ THE MIRROR BACKWARDS
READ THE MIRROR BACKWARDS

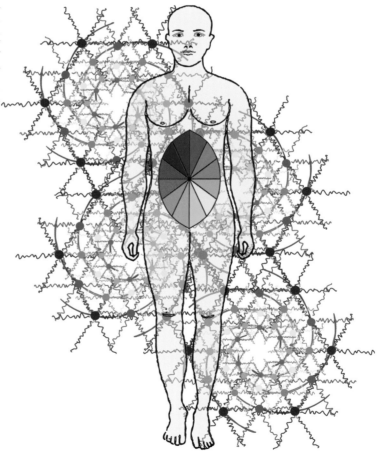

Practice this with an actual mirror in your reality to show the body how it works. The body is your ally, and of course, in our analogy, the body creates the *you* you know as your focus, your consciousness.

This may be a difficult idea for you to absorb, but apply THE LAW here and see the myriad of cellular combinations that construct the flat plane, linear illusion of your body.

See it too
as part of
a Spoke-Focus.

Each manifest
combination of a body
is not only the container of
a focus of consciousness,
it is that consciouness
itself,
made manifest.

64

Now, consider the idea that a multifaceted Spoke-Focus
is an accurate way to conceptualize reality.

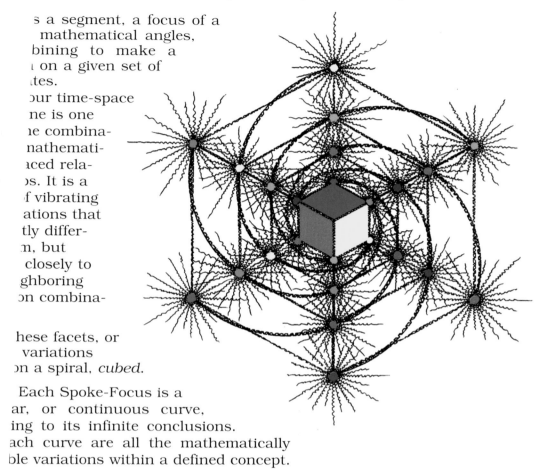

s a segment, a focus of a
mathematical angles,
bining to make a
ι on a given set of
tes.

ɔur time-space
ne is one
ιe combina-
nathemati-
ιced rela-
ɔs. It is a
f vibrating
ations that
tly differ-
n, but
closely to
ghboring
ɔn combina-

hese facets, or
variations
ɔn a spiral, *cubed.*

Each Spoke-Focus is a
ar, or continuous curve,
ing to its infinite conclusions.
ach curve are all the mathematically
ble variations within a defined concept.

For instance,
at its most simple,
one line will be a "1" series:
1, 2, 3, 4, 5 ad infinitum.
Another line will be even,
or odd number possibilities:
2, 4, 6, 8, 10 and so on.

This is an analogy, simplistic and
accurate enough mathematically to
ray the distinct and multivariable
ιre of the true curve differentiations,
accurate enough to make a point. In
ιality, no simple number system can
vey the intricacy of variation found in
ιutifaceted Spoke-Focus.

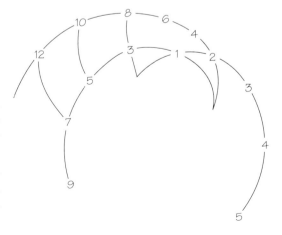

We are working here with a series of coordinates, in one sense, rigidly fixed by the definition limits set upon them; in another and truer sense, totally free-flowing and spontaneous, but interpreted or seen through the definition limits.

The curve on which any reality appears
is what mathematically predicts
the angle distortion's set of definition limits.

In other words, it is predictable as to how another reality will appear, once you know its curve coordinates. First you must find your own place on the curve of space, the Spiral of Creation. In the future this knowledge shall enter your earth reality, and then travel will be possible, on your own and on neighboring curves, energy lines, spirals on the Spoke-Focus.

Farther out, away from your familiar focus of coordinates it shall be difficult to travel, only because you will have no facility to see, hear, feel, or even sense the appearances of the new locale. In the beginning there will be the talented and brave few who will have the ability to *adjust their focus* and at least partially perceive other angle distortions as materializations.

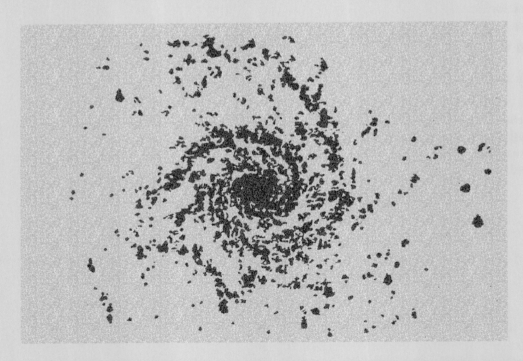

Here we extend on your time curve to a greater, farther future. Your earth appearance says "later," or "farther," because you seem to travel on a linear curve, yet it is all happening *now*, since *now* is the only true time definition.

AN ALTERNATE VIEW, OR, ANGLES ON THE SPOKE

apter Two tends toward the abstract, and the teachers' focus looks at
: are headed as we develop the mental abilities to travel and move along
es. However, the concepts that describe the cosmic level also work at a
level (as above, so below) and the following story from one of the stu-
THE EXPERIMENT illustrates another angle on the Spoke.

❖   ❖   ❖

poke-Focus was a concept I was having difficulty with. As a student of
ı Michaels I was being trained in the seemingly monumental task of
ging my beliefs about who I was and how the world worked. This is a
how I began to grasp one aspect of Spoke-Focus.

ı the summer of 1989, I went with an acquaintance to the San Geronimo
t Taos Pueblos. It is a very popular event and many native Americans as
non-natives attend. I was walking through the festival with this woman
ddenly exclaimed, "Did you see that?!"

asked, "What? What was it?" She then described a couple having an
ınt in which the man was shoving the woman. I tried to see this interac-
ıoking to where she was pointing, but I could only see people enjoying
ılves at the dance. I chalked it up to there being too many people in the
my vision and we went on.

As we were walking through the crowd again, I saw a *Koshare* (clown)
ʒ an Anglo woman and I pointed this out to the woman with me but she
ı't see it. I was a little dumbfounded as I could see it happening clearly
ʒh the crowds. She really could not see it, as I did not see her event. I then
to remember the lesson on Spoke-Focus.

As we walked on, a similar thing happened where she witnessed another
ıent and pointed it out to me but again, I couldn't see it. Now I was con-
ı that we were walking together in a common agreement that we were in
Pueblo at the dance, that the sky was blue, that we were seeing many peo-
common spoke on the focus) but that we were in different positions on the
: of this Spoke. We were really experiencing two different realities. It was
hat I just couldn't see through the crowd - it was that our perceptions were
ʳo different positions.

This experience continued throughout the dance and by the time we left,
ı an expanded view of a Spoke-Focus and how we truly perceive reality
ʳd on our position on the Spoke.

❖   ❖   ❖

Chapter Two is called The Shape of Reality because the Spoke-Focus
pe truly is the matrix through which we experience life. As the teachers say,
ıether you go backward or forward, in or out, up or down, larger or smaller,
always find another (Spoke-Focus). Each is an appearance of THE ALL."

We welcome <u>your</u> stories. Send them to us on our website,

www.theakademe.com

ı we'll try to make some of them available for others to read. In the mean-
ıe, Appendix C, p. 195, has some further thoughts on Spoke-Focus.

CIRCLES

In each full circle
Is a new beginning.
            In each autumn
            Is a spring.

                        From inches to miles
                        From moments to years
                            We circle the patterns of our lives
                            In variating curves
                                Of inner delights.

In each full autumn
Is a circling beginning.
In each spring
Is a now.

In laughter or smiles
In sorrow or tears
We pattern the circles of our lives
In curving variation
Of depth, width and height.

CHAPTER THREE
<u>CONSCIOUSNESS</u> <u>IS</u> <u>A</u> <u>CONSTANT</u>

The way light is refracted is the way
the mathematically proportioned angle distortions of earth's focus
create appearances, materializations.

REFRACTION
(L. re, AGAIN **+ frangere,** TO BEND, TO BREAK**)**

Refraction describes the way light is slowed down, bent or deflected when it passes from one medium, like air, into another medium of a different density, like water or glass. In FIG. A, the light is bent when it enters the prism and again when it leaves.

When light passes through a lens-shaped glass or the lens of an eye, the rays are all bent together and collected at a point, focused. Information encoded in the light becomes available to the brain, and an amazing thing takes place. *We see.*

If the light were not focused, (dotted lines in FIG. B), the information would go right by, unseen. The act of shaping the light transforms it, intensifies it, and at the point of focus, the visible world is created.

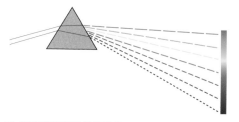

(A) REFRACTION THROUGH A PRISM SEPARATES WHITE LIGHT INTO THE SOLAR SPECTRUM.

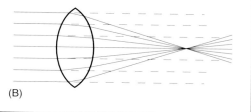

(B)

At times a shift of focus may cause a familiar scene to appear in a new and unfamiliar way. This is due to variations in focus. These angle distortions are changes in the angle of focus.

A series of related energy units, for instance sounds, colors, numbers, can appear as a tree in your reality, a song in another reality, and so on.

Our 3D earth reality exists as one facet in a multifaceted structure of realities. The angle of our position on the curve determines the way we perceive. Other realities exist which experience perception at differing angles and degrees of focus. We could all be "seeing" the same light from the same source, but focusing at different angles, creating various appearances.

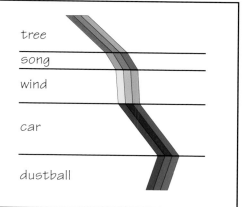

tree
song
wind
car
dustball

All energy is life, a joyfully spontaneous offshoot of the One Energy, and only focus, angle distortion, makes it appear as what you seem to see it as.

CONSCIOUSNESS IS A CONSTANT.

Energy units combine to create greater, more powerful units: variations. The way you define these combinations
(which is influenced by the mathematics of your place on the
curve) is the way you create the appearance of what you see.

This is not an accurate enough way
to explore your reality scientifically.

DO NOT READ THE MIRROR;

SEEK THAT WHICH REFLECTS
ONTO THE MIRROR.

Do not deduce from reading appearances
with the eye, for it sees only what the mind
defines it can and should see, within a set
of mathematically influential coordinates.

For instance, an energy unit
approaches. You hear a car, with a
motor, coming down the street
toward you, passing you and leaving your range of sight, hearing,
your senses.
This same energy unit
could be a wind, a rainbow, a
dustball, a song ... all seeming
to enter your range of sense
perceptors, enlarge and then
leave.

These are all illusions,
shaped by your definitions.

A rainbow would not
come down the street "making
noise", and then leave. Nor would
a dustball, but a car, by your definitions, does that, and so the energy
unit becomes CAR to you, because it fits
all your definitions.

You may hear a song. It begins, you listen to its linear progress and it ends. Perhaps the words create a series of mental images which, to you, do not seem to materialize, but you experience them internally as thoughts, emotions, pictures. This is another way an energy unit 'appears' to you, multilevelled and intricate, as the sounds, the notes, the instruments and voice combine with the words and images to create a full experience.

This same energy unit could appear to you as a dustball if it were constructed of a series of more distant coordinates - more distant to your time-space focus zone, and so you would hear no sound, see little color, give it no credit for a life of its own and easily dismiss it, hardly notice it.

Yet, if it appears in your reality, you know that this energy unit is within a certain spectrum of coordinates. That is why it appears within earth's visible range. It would otherwise be 'invisible.'

Realities run on different plane depths as well as on one-plane variables. You could say that the plane just in front of your here-and-now view, is more stretchable, fluid, liquid and variable, less rigid and fixed to your perception and definitions.

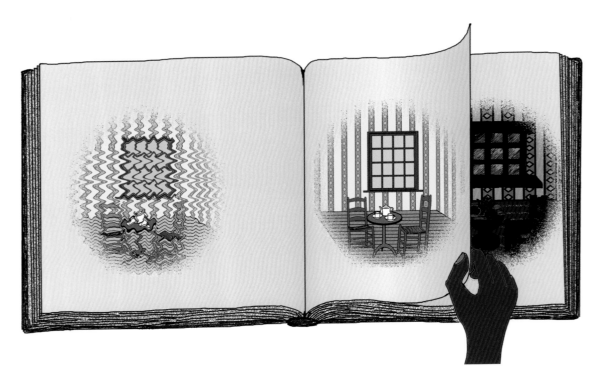

In the opposite direction, one step behind, it could be a more rigid, thicker, fuller, heavier, 'squarer' reality. This would be a variable on a line of perception, a differential of number coordinates of a 'seemingly linear' path on a curve.

Take a series of mathematical coordinates that to your perception can appear solid, such as our tea set.

Quantum experiments in virtual reality show that empty space is far from empty. It is filled with a seething profusion of 'virtual' particles which exist for a fleeting moment and are gone. Though any given particle can only exist for an inconceivably short period of time, the cloud of virtual particle energy is potentially infinite. It has even been speculated that the Universe may have originated from a random fluctuation in the virtual energy of the void . . .

Between each of the material objects that you do perceive are minute variations on the curve, where those combinations of coordinates do not appear as solid, or perceptible to you, but exist nonetheless.

In earth perception, you deal with differentials in solid number terms. These that we speak of are non-solid numbers.

Mentally, you can travel on a line of numbers, into squares and infinite fractions, but these are all still measures within the definition of solid numbers. What we discuss now are variations in non-solid numbers. Again, we are reading the *Reflector*, that which reflects on to the mirror: non-solid numbers. The mirror reflects this back to you as solid numbers (the *reflection*).

> SOLID: having length, width, depth, three dimensions.

As *solid* is what appears in your reality, you can perceive along a line of solid number variations. In other words, you can travel along this perceptible line of "one through infinity."

IMAGINE

IMAGINE THIS:

Think of the third dimension as a tube that you are moving through. In front of you the light is bright, the images are vaporous, thin and fluid. As you travel, the light from the beginning of the tunnel dims behind you in the distance.

The images in the tunnel get firmer, harder, clearer, until you reach the one spot where everything is crystal clear and in focus.

This spot marks your specific three-dimensional time-space earth reality.

Now you pass on further into the tunnel, and as it gets darker, the images are fuller, deeper. You are still in the tunnel, the third dimension, but your eyes are not accustomed to the darkness, and it is hard to see clearly. As your vision adjusts, you find you may catch fleeting images (of other realities) until you enter total darkness. Here you cannot see at all.

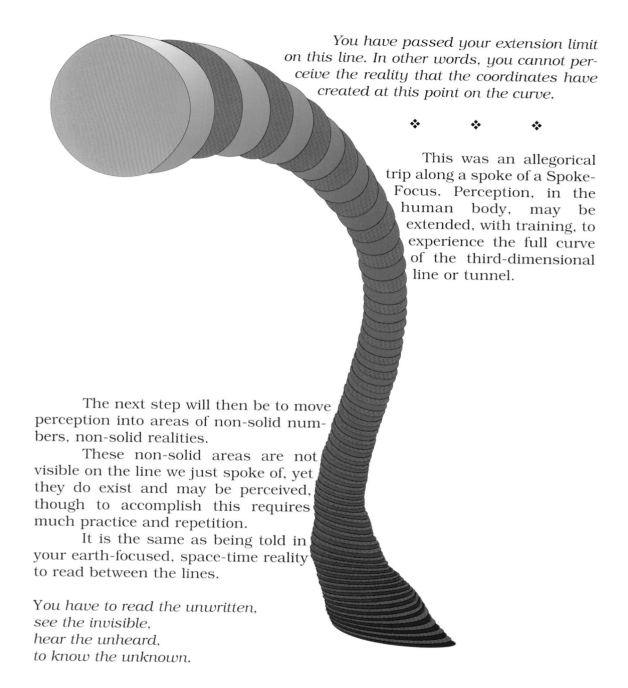

You have passed your extension limit on this line. In other words, you cannot perceive the reality that the coordinates have created at this point on the curve.

❖   ❖   ❖

This was an allegorical trip along a spoke of a Spoke-Focus. Perception, in the human body, may be extended, with training, to experience the full curve of the third-dimensional line or tunnel.

The next step will then be to move perception into areas of non-solid numbers, non-solid realities.

These non-solid areas are not visible on the line we just spoke of, yet they do exist and may be perceived, though to accomplish this requires much practice and repetition.

It is the same as being told in your earth-focused, space-time reality to read between the lines.

You have to read the unwritten,
see the invisible,
hear the unheard,
to know the unknown.

By accomplishing each of these you pass through a barrier that you have previously set up by your definitions of reality.

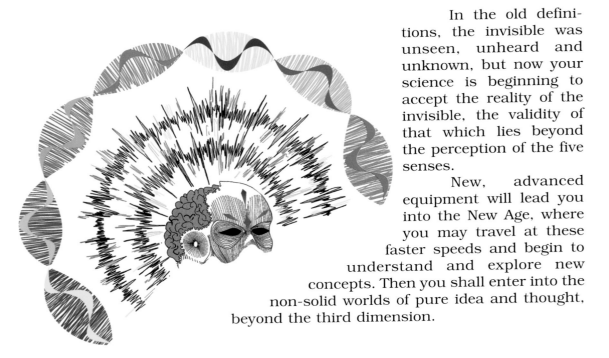

In the old definitions, the invisible was unseen, unheard and unknown, but now your science is beginning to accept the reality of the invisible, the validity of that which lies beyond the perception of the five senses.

New, advanced equipment will lead you into the New Age, where you may travel at these faster speeds and begin to understand and explore new concepts. Then you shall enter into the non-solid worlds of pure idea and thought, beyond the third dimension.

Music and math have always traveled into these realms, but now the conscious mind, self-directed, must take the leap, and enter into the invisible side.

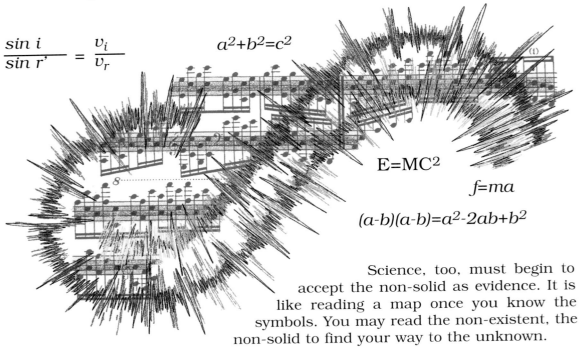

$$\frac{\sin i}{\sin r'} = \frac{v_i}{v_r}$$

$$a^2+b^2=c^2$$

$$E=MC^2$$

$$f=ma$$

$$(a-b)(a-b)=a^2-2ab+b^2$$

Science, too, must begin to accept the non-solid as evidence. It is like reading a map once you know the symbols. You may read the non-existent, the non-solid to find your way to the unknown.

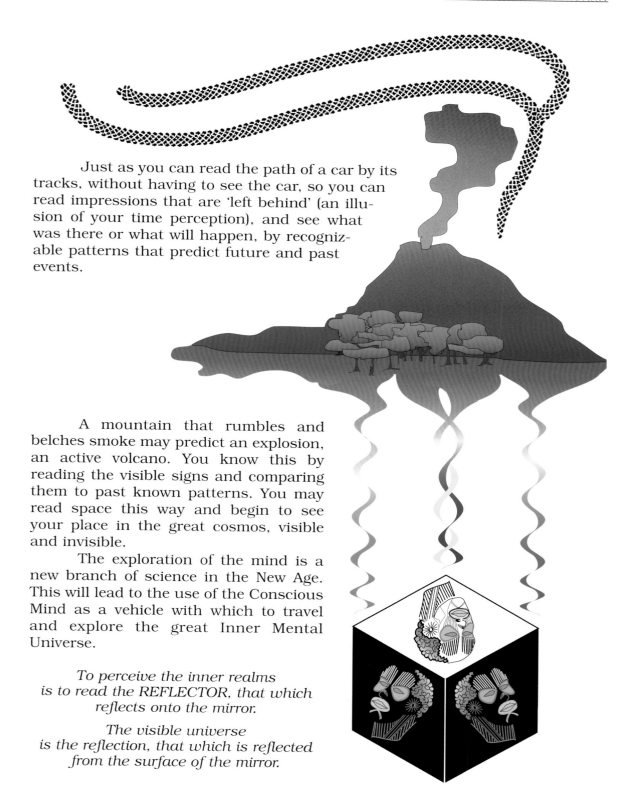

Just as you can read the path of a car by its tracks, without having to see the car, so you can read impressions that are 'left behind' (an illusion of your time perception), and see what was there or what will happen, by recognizable patterns that predict future and past events.

A mountain that rumbles and belches smoke may predict an explosion, an active volcano. You know this by reading the visible signs and comparing them to past known patterns. You may read space this way and begin to see your place in the great cosmos, visible and invisible.

The exploration of the mind is a new branch of science in the New Age. This will lead to the use of the Conscious Mind as a vehicle with which to travel and explore the great Inner Mental Universe.

To perceive the inner realms
is to read the REFLECTOR, that which
reflects onto the mirror.

The visible universe
is the reflection, that which is reflected
from the surface of the mirror.

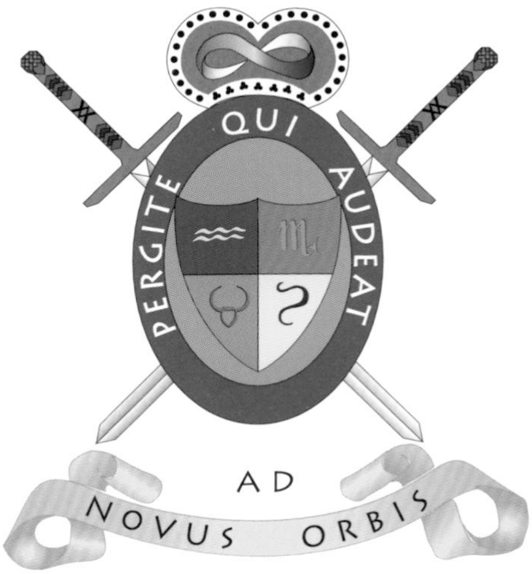
QUI
PERGITE
AUDEAT
AD
NOVUS ORBIS

Your reality's definitions must be changed; the rich soil of the human conscious mind can be trusted and explored. Explorations *in here*, in the inner realms will *not* uncover dark and hidden recesses of 'natural instinct,' supposedly destructive and uncontrollable (as the church and science have implied).

Instead you shall enter the open and as yet little explored wilderness of mental universes. This is your next horizon. The wide open spaces of humankind's mental resources await your first bold explorers.

Those of you who are not afraid of the monsters that roam the sea and devour ships (as you have been told the subconscious is), or of the sirens that lure you to your death on the rocks (as the church says desires are), may boldly sail forward, unafraid and confident, adventurous and exploring, looking for and finding far-off and exotic lands of delight and wonder

WITHIN.

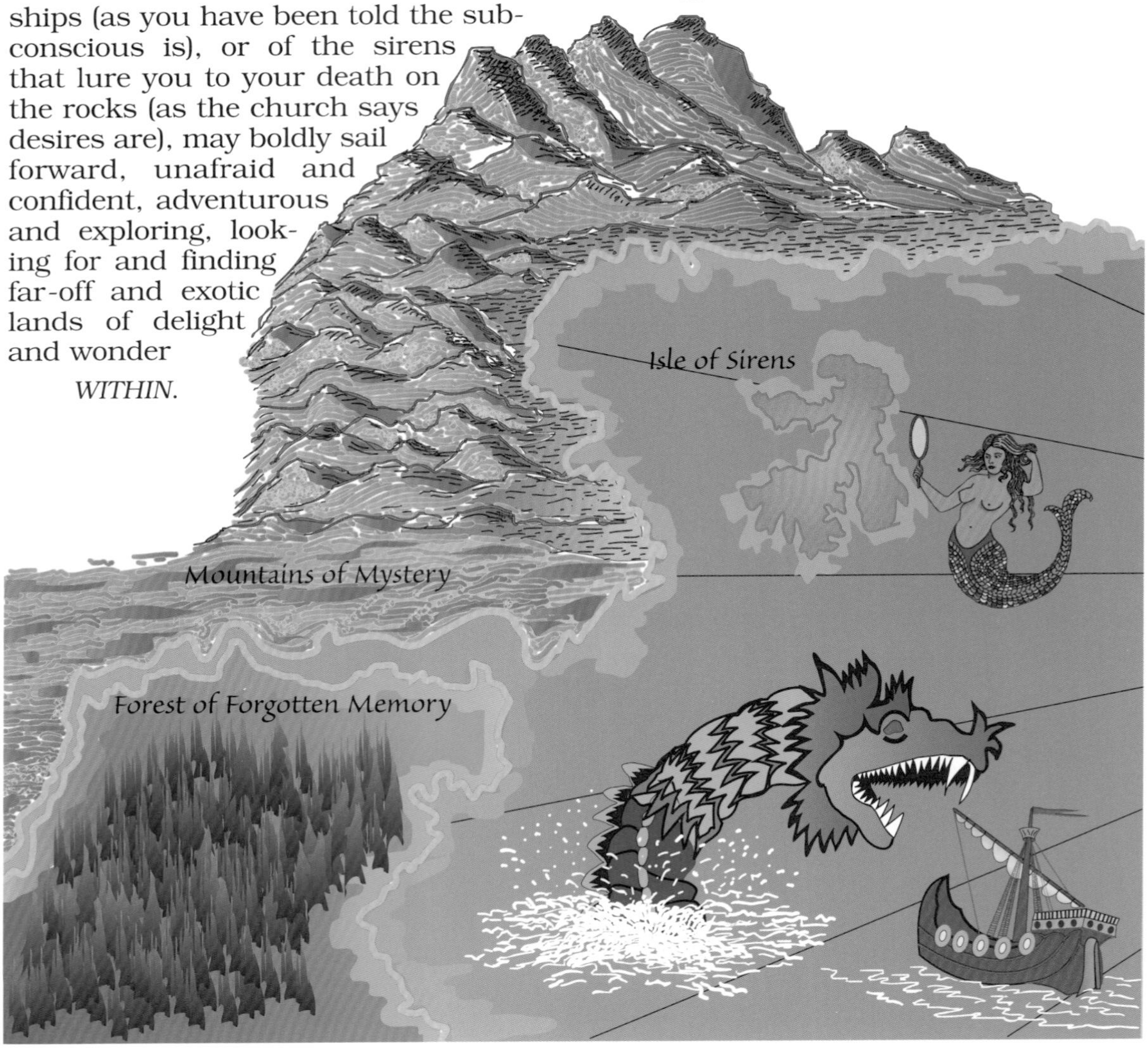
Isle of Sirens
Mountains of Mystery
Forest of Forgotten Memory

This is a journey on a linear curve, and we begin to seek out the neighboring and accessible non-solid realities.

Solid realities, like solid numbers, revolve around a core, an origin of non-solid realities, non-solid numbers . . .

just as colors revolve and spiral around a core of non-colors; which is to say that there are _core vibrations of non-three-dimensional co-incidence._

You must see the unseen to establish proof of hearing the unheard, which describes to you

the Unknown.

A clear definition of reality will, of itself,
realign racial and planetary definitions.

In other words, _Truth Will Out._

DOOMED

Truth is the great power that is often feared in your reality. This power, greater than the perceiver, is a harmonious and just power, built of a multicomplex of consciousness constructs, interacting, inter-being.

Consciousness, in your reality, is ready to discard the Dark Age definitions of humankind and its place in the universe.

Those misinterpretations and their manifest physical reflections will no longer be a part of your play, your song, your experience, your reality.

No longer will you be menaced by the threat of great, dark, powerful beings
who intend harm: devils, germs, the dangerous subconsciousness,
the dictators of unjust rule.

And as it was Written so it came to pass, that he was Smitten on the Tuberosity of his Ischium.

In the coming years you shall see the changes occurring, as they have begun: a new and bursting awareness of the precious and common-to-all gift of life that is within each on earth.

This knowledge is spreading, and Life will once again be recognized as miraculous, as the Divine within us.

This awareness is necessary if these new concepts are to be understood and explored. A basic respect for all life is needed if you come exploring the universes, inner and outer.

LIFE must be seen as THE ALL, joyfully, wondrously Being.

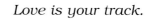

Love is your track.

If you follow it, it will lead you to a greater depth and awareness of our Multi-Being. Love is a current that you may use for constructing major highways to Inner Stars.

You need not call up love, nor squeeze inner emotional muscles to produce it.

Love is your electrical current. ALL THAT IS is constructed of units of this electromagnetic energy called Love.

When for a moment you are touched within by that sense of wonder, beauty and magic for your world, then for that moment the channel is open and clear, and you feel the Raw Power of Love.

There is nothing threatening or danger-ous about this Power.

This Power, greater than you, runs everything, IS everything.

That clear and enlightened feeling that comes when you look up and see the night sky, feel the wind or see the magnificence of the ocean, the mountains towering violet to your skies . . .

each moment of wonder and love for your earth and her magnificent creatures is *touching and being touched by* that Great Power Within.

Let go.
Be courageous,
unafraid.

Enter with confidence
The World of The Unknown.

85

PART TWO

<u>MINDSTRETCHING</u>

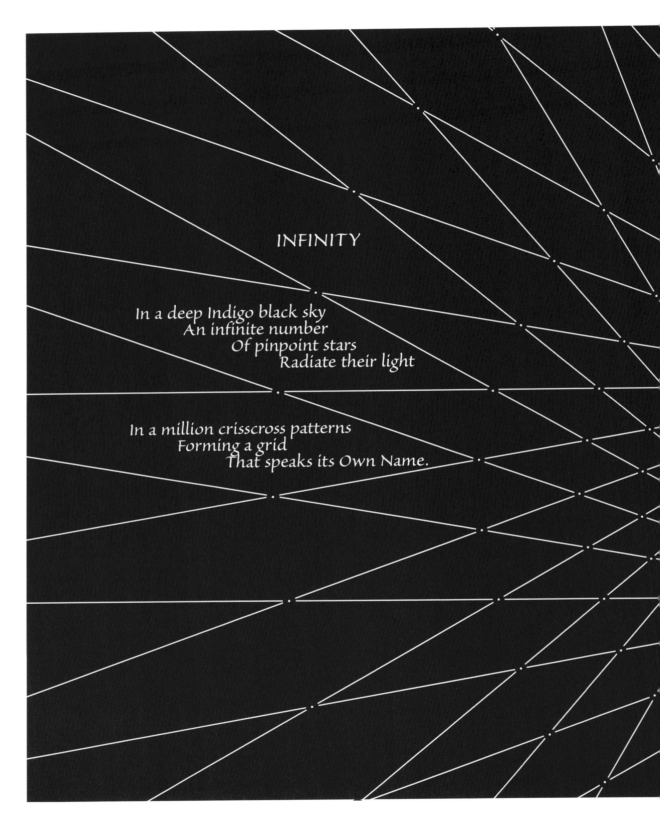

INFINITY

In a deep Indigo black sky
An infinite number
Of pinpoint stars
Radiate their light

In a million crisscross patterns
Forming a grid
That speaks its Own Name.

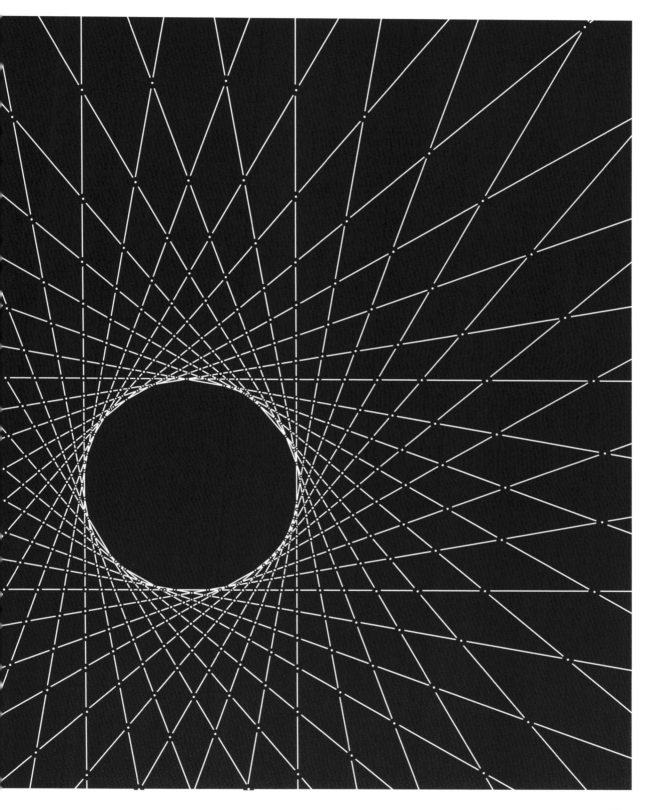

CHAPTER FOUR
THE <u>FLOW</u> <u>OF</u> <u>ENERGY</u>

MAGNETIC QUALITIES CREATE POLARIZATION.
POLAR OPPOSITES CREATE MAGNETISM.

MAGNETIC ENERGY MAY BE DIRECTED BY THOUGHT,
AND IF YOU CAN CHANGE THE POLES ON AN OBJECT
YOU CAN CREATE MOVEMENT
GREATER THAN THE PULL OF GRAVITY.

Since thought has magnetic properties, then the process involved in changing the magnetism of a thought is by thinking on a different pole. Basically simple. Simple enough for you to achieve proof of it by changing your thoughts, over and over, until proficiency allows actual movment. . . of basic definitions, of blocks of ideas, eventually of physical objects. That is a major part of this experiment in consciousness. Remember the Law of Polarity (Glossary): *opposites are identical in nature, but different in degree.* By thinking on a different pole, you are simply moving the emphasis along a scale of degrees - vastly simpler than attempting to change something's essential nature.

Of all the tools we have at our disposal for creating our reality, namely thoughts, words and deeds, thought is by far the most potent. It is our direct link with the Universal Mind. Through thought we define our reality and get in touch with our desires (the influences that reach us *from the stars*).

Thought shapes reality by a process known as accretion (the building up of material through attraction). This process is basic to the construction of form in time-space. It is the same process that brings a star into being. The material that forms a star is accumulated, bit by bit, around a center of attraction until the mass reaches a critical density and ignites.

A thought may come to mind that resonates with a deeply held desire - perhaps it shows a new approach toward achieving the desire. As we energize the thought with the force of intent, it becomes a center of attraction pulling in related thoughts, building a structure of our intent that will carry the thought into physical reality.

This is familiar to us - the conscious development of an idea into form. We do this in all creative endeavors. We may take an idea, a desire, and consciously develop it in this way, but far more pervasive and continuous is the way our habitual thought patterns and expectations magnetically attract related thoughts and images that, over time, develop such force that we unconsciously act out the pattern. This is, for the most part, what determines behavior and circumstance.

Behavior represents a natural extension of thought flowing from the mind, outward through the body and emotions, whereas circumstance is what *appears* to come from outside one's self, seemingly not the result of inner thoughts. This, however, is the consequence of living in a reflective reality. Remember - *reflection* means reversal. The thought patterns we energize ray out into the highly reflective medium of time-space and are reflected back as events and circumstances; *thought reflected into reality.* This is how "we create our own reality." That is why we continually experience our habitual expectations, be they expectations of success, happiness, sickness or failure. Edgar Cayce says that what we think continuously, we become. The thoughts that engage our attention day after day are built into the fabric of our bodies and reflect in our reality. Thus the person who lives in fear MAGNETICALLY attracts fearful situations; the one who dwells on the fulfilment of a long held desire MAGNETICALLY attracts that fulfilment.

When the individual becomes aware of this, she can take steps to consciously shape her own thoughts into patterns that reflect her truest and deepest desires. This type of mental manuever is the first step toward mastery of the MAGNETIC FIELDS of thought. When we learn to shape them to our advantage, they can guide us into realms of limitless potential, and that is the goal and the destiny of consciousness in THE EXPERIMENT.

Use the charts (the music charts and star charts, Appendix A, p.187) to align the MAGNETIC FORCES in the ether surrounding you. They may produce no visible effect, *in the beginning,* but the effects are there and they become visible over time. Note the changes that occur, around you and within you. You must live within a controlled construct by surrounding yourself with the charts. The energy lines within the charts meet at predescribed mathematical coordinates to create power structures, coordinate points, plugs where you can plug in mentally and receive an energy boost or flow.

This is analogous to the way energy lines that cross the earth meet at certain specific locations and combine to enhance energy, and to produce a flow, not unlike a spring of water that wells up out of the earth. This energy is intuitively sensed and these locations often become the sites of temples where people go to receive the spiritual energy, be they the Pyramids, Stonehenge or Mecca.

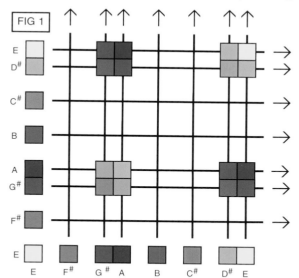

In the music charts the coordinate points where four color squares meet and create the 90 degree cross are POWER SOURCES (FIG.1).

Let us return for a moment to the concept that the Chart of the Key of E-Major creates the sound of the note of E. Within the chart are the energy coordinates, power sources, mathematically precise relationships between different rates of vibration. The energy-producing effect of the squares is created by their *vibration differences*.

> This principle of a differential, in physics and mathematics, is a well-established effect in which small differences between neighboring elements can produce significant movement.

Remember:
1. Opposites create movement.
2. Movement creates (the appearance of) opposites.
The first is reading the *reflection*;
the second is reading that which is reflecting onto the mirror,
the *Reflector*.

The mere coincidence of two different, not even opposite, vibrations together <u>WILL</u> <u>CREATE</u> <u>MOVEMENT</u>. On a scale of measure, opposites create more rapid movement, and mathematically proportioned differences in movement relate to the lesser or greater degree of angle relativity. The combination squares in the E Major chart are mathematically relevant. When you work with them, they will show you clear, simple relationships between number or color coordinates.

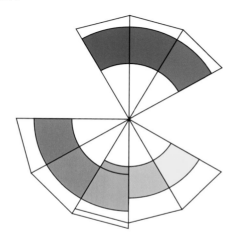

The chart produces power coordinate combinations in each primary color variation (see below). The E Major (yellow) chart produces one yellow combination (Y, Y-O, O), one red combination (R, R-O, O), and a blue combination (B-G, B, B-V). These combinations demonstrate clear, simple relationships between number and color coordinates, relationships that produce movement based on the principle of differentials. This occurs beyond the perception of the untrained senses, but is real and could be measured with the right equipment.

In other words, to create the sound of the note of E, you can produce the coordinate power squares of the E-Major chart. This, in turn, produces a series of energy lines extending, raying out, which ultimately create the sound of the note of E, first in the ether and then, it is possible, physically!

Do you understand this? By creating the power coordinates
you construct, make, align and sound the tone of E.

In my mind's eye I see a tile floor with these color coordinate squares laid out
on an otherwise white floor, and the room sounds the tone of E - almost audibly - but sensed
by the body as vibrating just beyond the range of human hearing. . . KM

You shall live in a house constructed thus, as it is a part of THE EXPERIMENT.

Begin to live with the charts projecting into the ether surrounding you, magnetically aligning you. Then observe the visible magic that grows proportionally within and around you.

You must live THE EXPERIMENT
to tell of it, to understand it,
to Be it.

By choosing your surroundings for their desired results you are creating a controlled construct which keeps you on track, directed. For just as the E Major chart creates the sound of the note of E, so your surroundings create you.

If this is difficult for you to understand, if you have spent years turning *within* to find the Reality behind the world of appearances, then be aware that what you call *without* is one area of control, and a very accurate medium to see THE REFLECTOR,

IF you do not read it as the *reflection*.

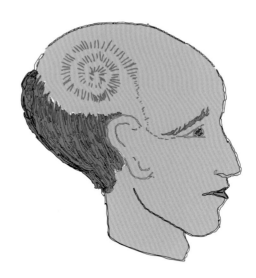

You *think* that you create your stage, your surroundings, your reality, from an awareness center within. You *see* it all through eyeballs from within the skull, where the awareness *seems* to be centered.

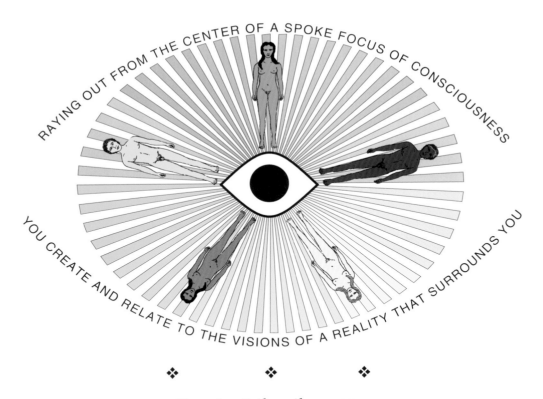

RAYING OUT FROM THE CENTER OF A SPOKE FOCUS OF CONSCIOUSNESS

YOU CREATE AND RELATE TO THE VISIONS OF A REALITY THAT SURROUNDS YOU

❖　　❖　　❖

Now, try it the other way.
Enter the three-dimensional field, the earth stage,
from the outer extensions and zero in to a single consciousness:
the *you* you are aware of.
If the whole creates the single
and the ALL creates the illusion of a one, a unit, (a sense of separation),
then the ALL, the myriad, the many create the one:

you.

One way to control or change the *you* awareness within is by exercising careful selection of the many things around you: the many objects, colors and sounds. You can MAGNETICALLY align the surrounding vibrations in your environment to obtain a desired result: a directed energy field in which you place yourself,

IN WHICH YOU CREATE YOURSELF!

This is today's concept. Read this over and over until it begins to take root in your information center, your subconsciousness. It will become a part of your correct interpretation of life on earth, your stage, your circumstances. It shall reflect on your mirror:

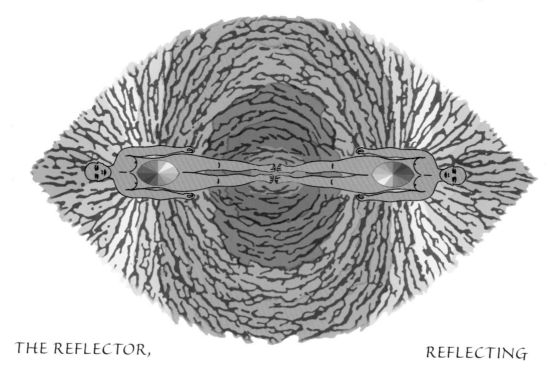

THE REFLECTOR,   REFLECTING

Monday June 23, 1980

It's now about 8:20 A.M. *Feeling a little tired from last night's dinner party. . . KM.*

Relax, child. This is a time of renewing and relaxing to build again, to build energy and personal power, to store the Power in you to replace depleted Power. Experiences like last night deplete you and waste stored power for brief moments of heightened perception. Is it worth it?

I answer that no, it isn't, and then, as they often do, the teachers used my experience to move into the day's lesson. . . KM

Think of your body (and the surrounding ether)
as a flexible, stringed instrument, able to sound
a multitude of infinitely variable combinations
of thoughts, feelings, emotions and moods.
The way you experience these variables
is how you play your *instrument*, your body.

This is the Greatest Art of the Musician:
playing the chords of your own being
in total ACCORD and harmony.

We are learning colors and their patterns of interaction
because, through the eye, you can play the keyboard
of your moods and feelings by looking at certain colors
or at the color charts of the keys of music.

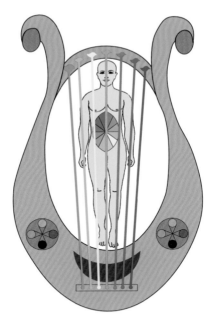

In other words,
you can affect the magnetic alignments
of your thoughts, moods and feelings,
and produce not only the desired result;
you may creatively and CONSCIOUSLY make yourselves
as a Composition in Living,
a Song of Being.

This is an art, long known on earth, then seemingly forgotten, to be revived and replayed on the New Instruments of the current human race.

You are made up of a series of mathematical quotients, groups of energy units that have the physical property of MAGNETISM, of attraction and repulsion, plus and minus. These energy units may be moved and manuevered, with awareness, into pleasing chords of interaction. One of the ways to effectively move them is with color, through the eye.

We are beginning to explore, through our discussions of the nature of mirror reflection, the art of directing thought. You will learn that to force anything to happen by squeezing the muscle of mental effort only brings into action the Law of Polarity (Glossary, p.202), the seeming bounce back that results in what you <u>don't</u> want. Focusing too strongly on the mirror, the outer appearance level, often brings into manifestation the opposite of the desired effect.

Instead, focus within on creating an image of the condition you want. Use your energy to produce as clear a mental image as possible without forcing anything. Then let the image go out into the ether. The reflection you want will inevitably follow. The success you have in this will depend largely on your ability to stay out of your own way. People often unconsciously interfere with what they want by thoughts of failure, or words that deny their own innate abilities.

The quality associated with the Tarot image of The Magician is *transparency*. The magician consciously determines what she wants and then lets the larger power flow through her to achieve her desire. The magician does not quibble about how, or when, or where the results must happen - she simply goes about her day in the calm certainty that her desires <u>will</u> manifest.

The importance of sound in creation must be carefully considered. Sound, shaped sound, is the power that brings energy into form. You shape energy by the words you choose to speak and by the thoughts (the silent sounds, unspoken words) you choose to dwell upon.

These choices, of images, of words, of thoughts, are some of the ways you manipulate, shape and form the energy coming through you. This is how you play your instrument, your personality, and much depends upon alignment. The <u>I Ching</u> has a line that says, in effect, that one experiences good or ill fortune depending on the forces with which one chooses to align.

Now learn the art of feeding the eye, the brain, the subconsciousness, with chosen vibrations known, by experience, to produce specific alignments. Feed the eye with the sounds of harmony, expressed in color. Use the charts, the music charts and the seven-star charts (see Appendix A, p 187) to produce alignments that will help you create a pleasing and fulfilling life sculpture.

Certain color vibrations are known by experience to produce specific, desired results, and you may choose the color combinations that enhance the three-dimensional properties you wish to emphasize.

On the solar spectrum, yellow sits in the middle with red to one end and blue toward the other end.

Consider the image to the right. What is the effect of taking the two extremes of the neutral color, yellow, and placing them together? The effect is MOVEMENT. Back and forth, the eye flicks chaotically between the red and blue. The movement is rapid. Actual heat is produced.

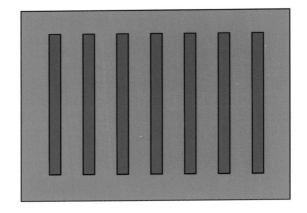

Are there MAGNETIC links
between colors?
Do some repel each other,
as the red and the blue in the diagram
seem to do?

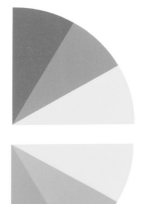

There is an ease of sliding from one color to its neighbor, for instance, from yellow to yellow green, or from yellow to yellow orange, depending upon the MAGNETIC alignment of the person observing the color. One person may have a personal prediliction toward yellow green, the blues, cool and fast, whereas another may lean toward yellow orange, the warm, slow reds.

Why does red, the slowest color,
produce movement,
and why does blue, the faster color,
have a calming effect?

Remember the mirror, the reversal.
Remember the Law of Polarity.
The ability to produce effects
must take into account
the workings of these laws.

Yellow holds the center. It is a non-moving color, and the standpoint from which you may produce effects. Blue is on the inward-moving cycle, the colors coming toward you. Red is on the outward cycle, with the colors moving away, and yellow is neutral, balancing. (In physics, an approaching light source is said to be blue-shifted, whereas a receding light source is said to be red-shifted. For more on the colors and their properties, see Appendix A on the color charts, p.187.)

We can produce movement on the emotional, feeling level by playing the keys of color. One of the first steps is to live with the colors and patterns and observe in yourself the results. First, observe the alignments that each specific chart produces and secondly, observe the specific colors and try to feel their properties.

The teachers paused here to advise me on how to renew myself by using the charts to recharge the cells of my body with balanced, healing energy by gazing at and meditating on the charts. . . KM

We will end the session shortly, as you are in need of recharging. Use the charts now, in this lower energy time, to store colors. <u>Feed</u> <u>the</u> <u>eye</u> <u>with</u> <u>balanced</u> <u>light</u>. This will charge the body with stored memory cells of aligned and harmonized color.

The eye takes in the color and the brain stores it, and, as an actual nourishment, the vibration reverberates through and is assimilated into the body.

Repeated seeing, feeding the eye, builds up a magnetic flow in the direction and pattern viewed until there is an extra amount that stays at a conscious level.

This is like filling up your body with color, until it overflows, so to speak, and spills out from within, to the surrounding ether. It is an inundation of aligned color, an internal bath in flowing, ordered vibrations.

We are building your inner space ship with color-aligned thoughts, words and deeds. As we proceed we will explore multivariables and inner space travel, as this is another way of consciously moving from one vibration level to another. We shall increase versatility and flexibility with *color travel* and then move into *reality travel*.

THE THREE FATES

Speak well of plans and woven threads
That name the path you seek.
Read clear the scroll that writes the way
The wanderer will reap.

The winding path of destiny
The lot that life bestows
    A length the warp and weave create
    Our nemesis that knows.

    In each reflection of a scale
    A seed to start anew
        To measure and give birth unto
        An alternating view.

Wednesday, June 25, 1980

It's now about 8:30 A.M. I had a really interesting dream about two mobiles in a museum. One was a "solar system" mobile. The planets were revolving in a series of concentric circles and each one was attached to the centerpoint by silver spokes. It was kind of a solar system Spoke-Focus. The other one, shown to me by the museum director, was truly incredible. It was a mobius strip that glided around, up and over walls and across the room. It was so large that the director had to move walls in the museum to make room for it. Amazingly, as he touched the walls to move them, they glided effortlessly apart. The mobius itself was a large, white strip that seemed to move not just up and over the walls, but somehow through them as well. It was spectacular. The planet mobile was $60 and the mobius was $4000. . . KM

CHAPTER FIVE
THE SHAPE OF THE FLOW

THE MOBIUS

The curve of space is like a mobius strip.

The curve you see through the crystal is the curve of space,

and like the mathematical symbol for infinity, the curve of space is a mobius strip.

CON-WITH SIDER-STARS
CONSIDER
WITH STARS CON SIDER

a ring made from a cosmic strip of paper. It surrounds an area of space and sets up a boundary that separates the inside from the outside.

For instance, a traveller on the outside surface of the ring will never get to the inside no matter how far she journeys (provided that she doesn't cross over the edge of the strip).

Because of these properties, the closed ring is symbolic of the limitations of the appearance of separateness.

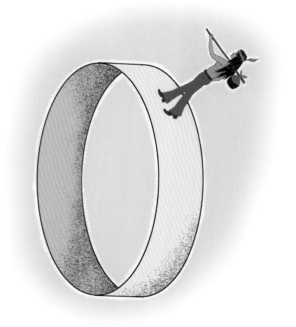

A mobius can be made from the same strip by putting in a half twist before attaching the two ends. This simple act is something of a magical transformation for the traveller, because although her perception at any given moment is still of a strip with two distinct surfaces (the one she is standing on and the one on the opposite, or under side of the strip), the mobius strip has removed the barriers that characterize the ring strip.

On the mobius, the traveller begins to walk along the surface, but instead of returning to the starting point after one revolution (as on the ring strip), she finds herself on the opposite surface, below her starting point. It is only after two complete revolutions that the traveller returns to the starting point and finds that she has traversed both the inside and the outside surfaces without ever having crossed over the edge. In fact the two opposite surfaces have become one.

Because of this, the mobius is a symbol for the type of perception
that sees the unity in the appearance of opposites.

Earth reality exists within a range of coordinates on the curve of space and that curve, earth experience, is mobius in nature. The mobius strip has two surfaces, but one continuous flat plane. One side represents the *Reflector*, and the other side the *reflection*. Perception is tuned to the physical environment, the *reflection*. The *Reflector* is the invisible side, the other side of the mobius, but its energy forms or creates the earth experience.

These two sides of the mobius are opposites of each other, like red and blue are opposite (as seen from the center, yellow). From the *reflection* they appear as opposites, but in actuality, the appearance of two sides is the result of the movement of the *Reflector*.

Remember the Law - <u>*movement*</u> <u>*creates*</u> <u>*the*</u> <u>*appearance*</u> <u>*of*</u> <u>*opposites.*</u>

Each mobius is a mathematical probable of motion variables, a specific frequency combination, that which reflects on the mirror. Each mobius is a Spoke on the Focus. They join at the center, so:

The flowers you are always drawing all your life have been shades, reverberations, echoes of the energy vision being pulsed through you.

The concept of the mobius blurs the boundary between visible and invisible. The physical mobius strip made of paper shows how, by a simple twist, the seemingly hard and fast qualities of three-dimensional space-time are mysteriously transformed. The rigidity of the *reflection* wavers for a moment, and a glimpse of the *Reflector* opens up. (Mathematicians who study topography, a difficult and complex field that deals with the properties of surfaces, know that introducing a twist into a surface can result in profound transformations.)

The mobius determines the shape of what you call earth reality. At any given moment, you seem to be standing on one surface of the mobius (the *reflection*), surrounded by compelling physical evidence that the world is solid and that the laws of cause and effect are comfortably in operation. However, when the energy travels to the *Reflector* side of your reality strip in the mobius energy field, the vision of your three-dimensional, solid reality seems to disappear, or become invisible. It's not that something travels a distance from you, away, down the mobius strip. It is rather that its energy field changes, moves to a frequency of vibration that becomes invisible; it has just entered the field of the reversed side of the mobius. This is not much different from the way that an audio frequency that changes to a rate of vibration beyond the range of hearing becomes inaudible.

The purpose of THE EXPERIMENT is to become aware of the *Reflector*, even if you can only "see" the *reflection*. As you stand on this side, surrounded by the evidence of the three-dimensional world, remind yourself of the existence of the other side. If you remember that everything you see is a *reflection*, a part of you will automatically note that a *reflection* must have a source, and that source is the *Reflector*. This may seem like a minor point, but it is a step in rebuilding your definition base to include an awareness of the invisible. As noted, when your definitions change, the world changes in response. By taking this small step, you consciously open a channel to the invisible side of the mobius, a channel that allows a two-way flow. In time you may keep one side of yourself grounded in physical reality while the other side consciously travels and explores the other side of the mobius.

In the dream, you (Ketherin) saw representations of our two sides, the Reflector and the reflected (the two mobiles). The planets extending in rays, silver bars from a nucleus, that is the reflected, 60, Michael - "a prop," just like a stage prop.

Here the teachers are using the language of Tarot to descibe the dream symbols. In the dream, the planet mobile was $60. Sixty, in Tarot, is the number value of card 14 which pictures the Archangel Michael. The meaning of the Hebrew letter associated with that card is "a prop." What the teachers are pointing out is that our view of the solar system, planets revolving around the sun, is a stage setting. . . KM.

The second mobile, the moving mobius channeled into walls, in defined and specific channels - that was the Reflector. The wall that had to be moved is the wall or barrier that separates the two sides of the mobius, the visible from the invisible. The museum office is the invisible side, the consciousness located above, within the brain and the visible side is the museum display area, the earth stage setting.

The ease with which the walls moved shows the mobility you have achieved in reaching the other side of yourself. The two (areas) became one and you brought the vision "home" with you. You brought the memory of the lesson <u>on the other side, the under side of the mobius.</u>

I could tell that the teachers were pleased with what I had accomplished and in my life, the dream was a turning point. The experience echoed, or reverberated through the years and became a symbol of my journeys with the teachers, around the concept pool. The significance of the number 4000, the price of the mobius mobile, comes again from Tarot. Four hundred is the number value associated with card 21, "The World," an image that represents Cosmic Consciousness. 400 x 10 is 4000, and is that consciousness, mobius consciousness, infused throughout the manifested universe. . . KM.

Now, to return to the mobius. The change over from visible *reflection* to invisible *Reflector* takes place within a predictable field of mathematical coordinates. That is to say, the mobius energy shifts, changes between solid and non-solid. We are entering an abstract area here. This is not a simple switch between positive and negative that we are describing. That would be a switch between two poles on a horizontal line with the visible on the positive side and the invisible on the negative side (FIG 1).

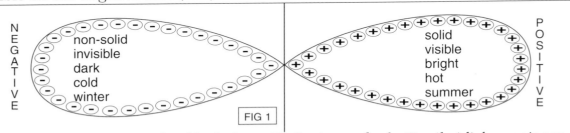

NEGATIVE

non-solid
invisible
dark
cold
winter

solid
visible
bright
hot
summer

POSITIVE

FIG 1

Earth perception is comfortable dealing with the types of polarities that link or pair certain qualities together. We tend to link daytime, visible, solid with the positive polarity while associating nighttime, invisible, non-solid with the negative polarity.

Mobius consciousness requires that the two-way polarity (positive to negative, or visible to invisible) be seen instead as a four-way construct. On the side where you link solid to visible there is a positive and a negative: positive/solid and negative/solid. On the other side, where non-solid is linked to invisible, there is the same: positive/non-solid and negative/non-solid. The four-way construct then becomes plus plus (++), positive/solid, plus minus (+-), positive/non-solid, minus minus (--), negative/non-solid, and minus plus (-+), negative/solid.

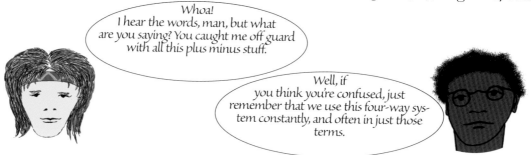

Whoa! I hear the words, man, but what are you saying? You caught me off guard with all this plus minus stuff.

Well, if you think you're confused, just remember that we use this four-way system constantly, and often in just those terms.

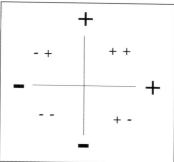

Consider the four-way construct called the Cartesian coordinate system developed by the renaissance philosopher and mathematician, Rene Descartes. It is used every day to make graphs, to plot equations, to give directions, to read maps; its uses are endless and familiar. This system divides any area into four quadrants by placing a horizontal line over a vertical line to make the crossbar shape shown at right. The area above the horizontal line is positive and below is negative. To the right of the vertical line is positive and to the left is negative. The four quadrants thus become upper right, plus plus (++), lower left, minus minus (--), upper left, minus plus (-+), and lower right, plus minus (+-).

You don't have to be a mathematician to get this. The practice of dividing a known quantity or quality into four quadrants is the way that the cycles of life are ordered. There are four seasons in the yearly cycle, four phases of the moon's cycle, four cardinal points of the compass, four parts to the cycle of light and darkness in a day.

To put this into perspective, consider the diagram of the four phases of the moon. It's easy to see that the full moon can be considered to be in the plus plus (++) area since it is the peak of the moon's size, brightness and visibility. Similarly, the new moon, dark and invisible, can be said to fall in the minus minus (--) area. The first and third quarters are in-between areas, partly visible and partly invisible so they become the plus minus (+-) and the minus plus (-+) areas. The same can be done with the four seasons and with the cycle of day and night.

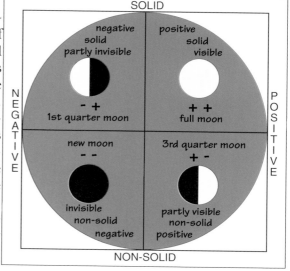

So how do we get from the Cartesian coordinate system to the mobius?

Let's take a look at the course of one day and night. To a personality based in linear time, the day appears to progress smoothly from one moment to the next. But if you superimpose the mobius onto the coordinate system, you can see the four aspects of day and night folding in and out of our visible field, and the in-between periods of dusk and dawn are the times when the mobius shift is most visible.

Look at the diagram below. Traverse the circle clockwise beginning with the quadrant on the upper right, daytime. This is the plus plus area (++). As you move from daytime to dusk, from positive/solid (++) to positive/non-solid (+-) there is a twist in the mobius. If you work within the mobius analogy, you could say that when the strip twists, the ++ energy (daytime) moves to a frequency of vibration that becomes invisible. It has entered the field of the reversed side of the mobius and disappeared from sight. As the one field (daytime) shifts into invisibility, another energy field becomes visible, the field of twilight, or dusk. The same thing happens when nighttime changes into dawn.

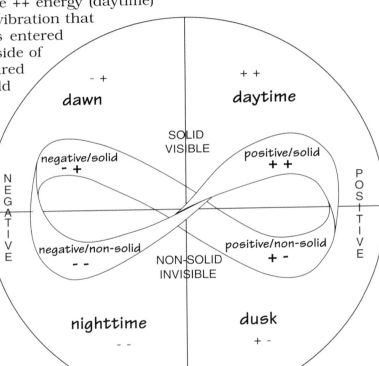

dawn - +

daytime + +

SOLID VISIBLE

negative/solid - +

positive/solid ++

NEGATIVE

POSITIVE

negative/non-solid - -

positive/non-solid + -

NON-SOLID INVISIBLE

nighttime - -

dusk + -

Wait a minute. What's the big deal? I mean, the sun goes down, it's dusk! The sun comes up, it's dawn! How do you keep track of all the shifting, twisting energy fields?

It's true that the earth description works O.K., but in the new millennium human consciousness is moving beyond the Newtonian, determinist view to a more flexible focus.

The plus and minus terminology is a bit abstract but bear with us as we lay the foundation for moving awareness into what we call the *four facets of focus.* (see Gossary, p. 202, see also 10 triangle design, p. 147 and 189)

The mobius is a device that integrates the visible and invisible sides of earth experience. Mobius consciousness reminds the awareness operating in three-dimensional space-time that the "other side" is not separate from this side: the mobius has two sides, but one continuous surface. Developing mobius consciousness can be as simple as remembering to see the "other side" of visible events. Following the mobius energy shifts or twists can be an enjoyable part of the life experience.

Corvus and I had fun watching, or observing, the visible and invisible sides of the seasons. Early on, before the actual book began, we were being told to adjust our view of the yearly cycle and switch from the standard and familiar Western view of the seasons as beginning with the Equinoxes and Solstices (top calendar). Instead, the teachers urged us to use the less familiar Eastern (Chinese) and ancient view of the seasons. In this view, the Equinoxes and Solstices, instead of marking the beginning of the seasons, mark instead, the midpoints of each season.

*As an example, the Summer Solstice, June 21, would mark the midpoint as opposed to the first day of summer. This corresponds to the calendar in the time of Shakespeare when the Summer Solstice was called Midsummer's Day, and celebrated as the height of summer. On the traditional western calendar, the upright cross is oriented to the Solstices and Equinoxes and to the beginnings of each season (top calendar). On this alternate calendar (below) used by the Greeks, the Celts and still used by the Chinese, the upright cross marking the beginning of the seasons shifts to a 45 degree **X** formation that is oriented to the midpoints between the Solstices and Equinoxes. In a season that lasts twelve weeks, this shift moves the beginning of each season forward by about six weeks to begin on or about the 1st to the 7th of February, May, August and November. In the Celtic calendar these dates correspond with the feast days of Imbolc, Beltane, Teltane and Samhain.*

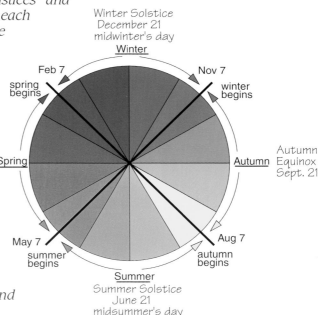

The reason, we were told, for such a necessary and radical change was that our Western definitions only took into account what was visible, and therefore never even considered the invisible side, the other half of each season. As we practiced and observed, it soon became very obvious that the change of season was actually evident on the four X points.

Each year, around February 7th or so, the whole feeling and tone of the weather, and even the mood of the world, would shift and spring would be visible. Not full-blown spring but merely the beginnings of spring: hints, whispers, signs. Watching for the signs of the seasons became a large, enjoyable part of our yearly observations.

Yes, we got the point our teachers were making. We, in typical Western fashion, were leaving out the invisible side, the other side, the inner side so that we were not operating with full knowledge. This rule applied to many aspects of our lives, and we were being instructed to readjust all of our calculations so as to include the Other Side, the "in here" side, the place and the knowledge found in the silence, within our Selves. . . KM

This knowledge of "the dreamer" or "the double," the other side, has cycled in and out of the earth experience, sometimes practiced by large groups of people (Atlantis, ancient Egypt) and sometimes kept alive by a few (the Essenes, the Nagual lineages described by don Juan), but always there, if only on the edge of the mass consciousness. The New Age is a time when that knowledge surfaces again, and THE EXPERIMENT is one of the many streams of information helping to bring it back to the forefront of the group attention.

The non-solid side of the mobius field of energy is the *dreamer*, the *double*, the *astral*, the *other side*. All these names are just ways of describing the energy related to the other side of your energy field, the other side of your Spoke on a Spoke-Focus.

You can sense, feel and know the invisible side - the only thing you can't do, without practice, is see it. The evidence is there for the finding if you do not rely on eyesight as proof. That is the only thing that stands in the way.

If the ear hears something, you do not always demand visual confirmation to prove its reality. If you hear or feel something, you often say it exists even if it is too distant, or too small, or too fast to be seen. Here also, there is a side of the mobius that can't be seen because it is in another frequency zone, too fast, too distant. These words describe vibration rates that are 'too' ? for you to see - only you have no word for 'too' what.

TOO MOBIUS - how's that?

We could call it TOO MOBIUS when energy enters
the other side of the energy field,
your Spoke-Focus, and becomes invisible.

This comment gave rise to one of those raucous bursts of humor on the part of the group of teachers. The tall man seated on the wall was banging on his pots and pans; others were laughing and yelling, "That's right! We're too mobius for most people to see us!" The challenge, sometimes implied, sometimes stated, is for the readers of THE EXPERIMENT to become skilled enough in travelling on the invisible side, the other side, to be able to contact the teachers on their own. The next chapter will begin the training in building and using the inner spaceship. . .K.M.

In the section on Light and Color, in the introduction, we put in a diagram of the spectrum of electromagnetic radiant energy. Take another look at that here.

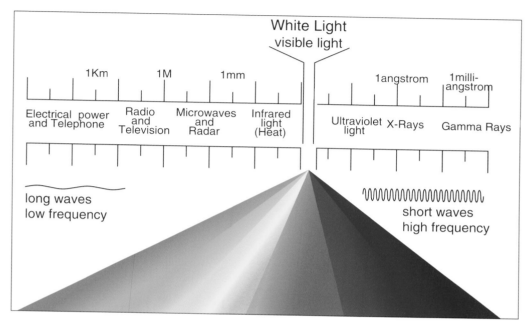

Notice how the rainbow spectrum of visible light originates from one point on the larger spectrum of energy, and rays out to command the field of vision. The diagram is analogous to the way that visible light, although limited to one octave in sixty, dominates the field of our perception to such an extent that the invisible fields of energy that surround us become unnoticed, or fade from significance.

The invisible side of the mobius represents the part of us that extends far beyond the limits of visiblility. Just as the light we see by is a minute fraction of the full range of energy, our bodies and our conscious awareness have been held to a limited view by our definition structures.

As we mention in Appendix C, p.195 on the Spoke-Focus, every cell, every atom of our bodies is in contact with every other part of the network of consciousness that makes up the Cosmos. Our extensions reach throughout this network, and, with practice, we may train the conscious mind to become aware of worlds beyond our sense of vision.

THE GREAT EQUALIZER

We start our story on a southern shore
And see the cliff's proud face.
    We hear the wind's small whisper.
We shall begin to trace
The movement of the earth
    In a race with other stars
To level all our mountains
And raise our valleys far
So they meet in equal measure
    The dwindling peaks of stone.

We meet the Great Equalizer
The Wind That Enters Bone.

Day by day, in now by now
The passing wind will take
    A minute piece of cliff with it
    And narrow down the gate
As one by one, invisibly
It carries sheer away
    The noble face of the rising cliff
    As it shifts another day,
And one step closer to nothingness
One atom nearer not
    A billion nows rush madly past
    The cliff, it is forgotten.

The cliff's short life, eternal years
Is only one small part
    Of a spectrum of what was visible
    In that one earthly spot.

Did the cliff leap boldly into the sea
And tear itself apart?
    Or did the gentle wind, the Penetrator
    Reach into its very heart and lift it
Piece by granite piece, up into the air,
    And gently drop it to the sea
        To mildly settle there?

The spectrum of the cliff is past
And now it is no more.
    It cradles warmly bright red crabs
    As they wade in from the shore
That is no longer shadowed
Nor protected by the cliff
    But is warmly baked and gently raked
    By the wind which brought this shift
        From high to low, from there to here.
        No matter, all is One.

The Great Equalizer, the Gentle Wind
        Creates the Fragile Bone.

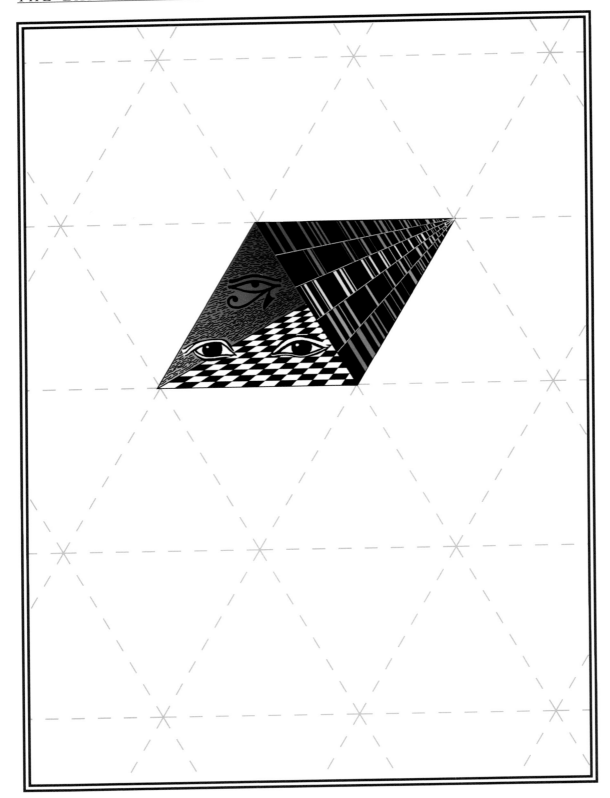

CHAPTER SIX
<u>TRIANGULATION</u>

Let us consider for a moment what is meant by *angle variance*. Angle variance is the degree on the curve of space at which a point manifests. A thought, an object, a reality. . . any or all of these are located at varying degrees on the curve of space, the mobius, and the inner space traveller may choose, at will, any angle variation desired, to achieve specific results.

> *The angle variance of a point is what determines how that particular point in time-space appears, because of its mathematical coordinates.*

THIS SIMPLE CONCEPT EXPLAINS ALL VARIATIONS IN APPEARANCE.

To enter the energy field of the mobius with control and work with something, we must take into account, know, and map its exact angle variance. As an example, we can locate a color from the spectrum of visible light. For instance, a decision as to the exact mathematical location of the hue of blue-violet on the scale of perceptible light frequencies gives us one point in finding its angle variance (FIG 1).

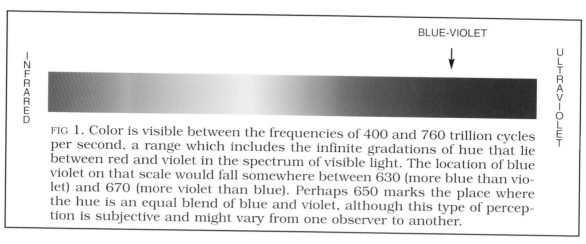

FIG 1. Color is visible between the frequencies of 400 and 760 trillion cycles per second, a range which includes the infinite gradations of hue that lie between red and violet in the spectrum of visible light. The location of blue violet on that scale would fall somewhere between 630 (more blue than violet) and 670 (more violet than blue). Perhaps 650 marks the place where the hue is an equal blend of blue and violet, although this type of perception is subjective and might vary from one observer to another.

This locates the color, or hue, but since it tells nothing about the other qualities, we must have more than one point to locate it. Relate it to three points, three areas of comparison with other known scales of measure, then TRIANGULATE to fix its position (FIG. 2, following page).

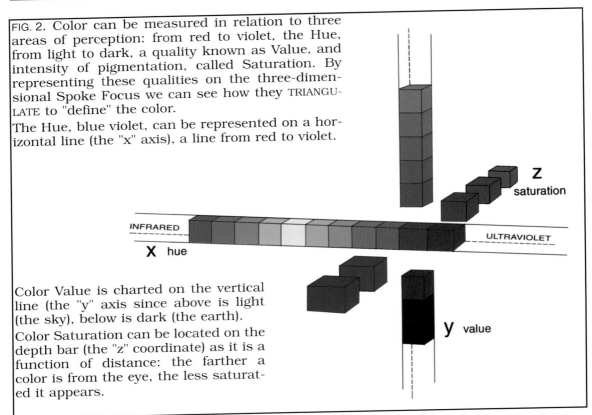

FIG. 2. Color can be measured in relation to three areas of perception: from red to violet, the Hue, from light to dark, a quality known as Value, and intensity of pigmentation, called Saturation. By representing these qualities on the three-dimensional Spoke Focus we can see how they TRIANGULATE to "define" the color.

The Hue, blue violet, can be represented on a horizontal line (the "x" axis), a line from red to violet.

Color Value is charted on the vertical line (the "y" axis since above is light (the sky), below is dark (the earth).

Color Saturation can be located on the depth bar (the "z" coordinate) as it is a function of distance: the farther a color is from the eye, the less saturated it appears.

These three points, hue, value and saturation, locate the angle variance of the color blue-violet on the three-dimensional curve, your earth reality, your specific location in time-space.

Raying out from the third dimension in a Spoke-Focus of varying angles and degrees, we find a vast area of possible worlds all operating within the medium of variable time-space; variable because in this fluid area, this playground, this medium of construction, all things are possible.

As all vessels are possible in clay, so all realities are possible in time-space. Time-space is the medium, the workable, moldable fluid of matter, of being, with which you work, play, and construct.

TRIANGULATION is one way we locate things. An address, for instance is a common form of triangulation. The street, a line extending in two directions, gives us one reference point. The street number provides a cross point along the line, the second reference. The third reference point locates the entrance which could be at ground level or it could be on the tenth floor, 120 feet above ground.

These three points always fix the *location* since a building doesn't move about in space; but it does move through time. This brings us to the *fourth point* - in arranging a meeting, we usually specify a location and a time. This fourth point is variable.

Finding the right location for an event involves triangulating on the proper spot; being there at the right time could be called *quadralating* since it requires us to consider a fourth coordinate as well.

The angle variance of time and space gives you two points to identify your place within this medium. Time is one line of measure. The movements of the sun, moon and earth give you coordinates to help you find your place on this line (ie. one rotation of the earth marks a day, one revolution of the earth around the sun marks a year). Scientists are beginning to locate your position in a partially constructed map of space. When they include the invisible as well as the visible, they will be able to determine your correct place within the map. There is a third point (SF, Subjective Focus) to be considered along with time (T) and space (S), one that we will discuss later (in the next book) as it is a more advanced concept.

The process being probed here is finding the angle variance of an object, a being, a thought, a color, a sound, anything at all, by TRIANGULATING on three points, by comparing the thing in question to three known areas of measured being.

For instance, the three lines of length, width, and height that define three-dimensional space are the three lines that define a cube from within; these three lines are also associated with the elements of fire, water, and air, which combine in creating the fourth. . .

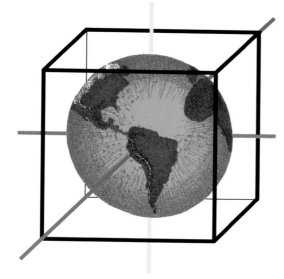

the earth,
the cube.

From the side of the REFLECTOR,
the fourth is invisible.
From the side of the REFLECTION,
the fourth is the earth.
Simple.

The invisible creates the visible.
The other side creates your side.

"You" are the reflected and you may gain control over your circumstances, your reality, your mirror, by working from the other side, which is reached from within. Always within.

Everything out there on earth that is visible is a clue, to reveal the invisible side. Go within to where it is all invisible to the two outer eyes . . . but visible with the third eye,

WITHIN.

The third eye is one point of three. This third point needs to be added to the two outer eyes (one a plus and one a minus) to give you a working formula. Then you may proceed, and experience what this triangulation will reveal to you.

Two eyes on earth give you the flat-plane appearance of things. Add the third point, the third eye, the Inner Eye, and a new depth is added to your earth experience.

The use of the third eye can help us tap into the potential of the mind and its physical vehicle, the brain. We are all well trained in using two eyes to see the physical world of objects.

[OBJECT: That which is put, or placed, in the way of the senses.]

But what of that which is not '*placed in the way of the senses?*" Cosmology, the study of the origins of the universe, has at times theorized that 90% to 99% of the substance in the universe may be invisible, the so-called "dark matter." Brain research tells us that at our average current development we use from 1 to 10% of our brain capacity. Is there a connection?

The invisible world is all around us. Using the third eye along with the two physical eyes opens or expands the capacity of the brain to receive and process information from the invisible side.

This all must be experienced on earth, to be known, to be enjoyed, in THE EXPERIMENT.

REMEMBER
RENEW

We may locate any
angle variance
coordinates
by TRIAN-
GULAT-
ING.

TRIANGULATION is a powerful tool used in radio astronomy, navigation, surveying - all types of mapping and exploration. It can be used to locate objects in space, or, in the example of the color blue violet, it can locate a subjective experience (the perception of color). Now let us consider a TRIANGULATION between the outer eyes and the inner eye as a tool to explore beyond the flat-plane interpretation of reality.

When THE EXPERIMENT states that the two eyes on earth give you a flat-plane appearance,

that although we live in three dimensions of space, earth dwellers are, for the most part, oriented around flat planes. Everything that we do, from birth to death, depends upon the myriad of flat planes we use, from floors to roads, to tables, to books, to beds. . . the list is endless.

The two eyes are so habituated to seeing a flat-plane version of reality that few people visualize in three dimensions. One clue perhaps is that anything we see in the world of objects can be effectively rendered onto flat planes through photography, drawing, painting, video, etc.

Another clue is that normal vision is a TRIANGULATION between three points - the eyes, (points one and two), and a third point, the point of focus. Three points, in Geometry, is the mathematical definition of a flat plane.

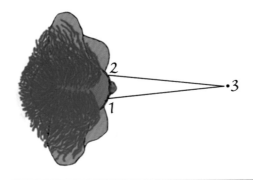

In the world where gravity holds us to the flat plane, three points is the basis of stability and support.

Yogis and others say that when we look with the eyes, a ray or beam of energy flows through the eyes and magnetically links our perception to the plane of appearances. This beam interacts with other beams to create an energy network that is seen as the flat-plane world of outer appearances.

This link is the basis of our collective agreement that what we see, the *reflection*, is the real and only world. When turned outward, the two eyes can then see only the single agreed-upon earth reality (a lamp post is always a lamp post).

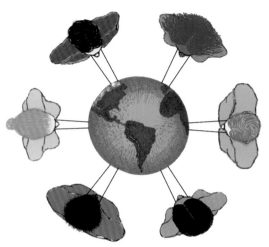

When the beam is used exclusively for flat-plane viewing, the outer world becomes the only world and the beam becomes an anchor holding the mind to the same view, much like gravity holds our bodies to the surface of the earth.

In each case, the perceiving mechanism is so focused within a closed system of perception that no other view seems possible, a condition called in THE EXPERIMENT *mirror blind* or the *two-eye view*. Consider the following flat-plane paradox.

Mathematically and topographically, the surface of the earth is a closed system - it curves around to meet itself. Therefore, the traveller that sets out across the surface of the sphere in a straight line must eventually end up, in the future, at a point behind where he or she began the journey. In the two-eye view, we accept this type of paradox as normal, or "just the way it is."

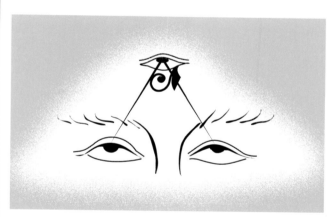

The same energy that creates and maintains the two-eye view can be turned to focus Within to engage the power of Inner vision. We will not be so naive as to expect a few exercises to give us mastery of the power of the third eye. In this, as in all things, mastery takes a lifetime or perhaps many lifetimes, but, although its use has not been encouraged in western culture, the power of Inner vision, or the third eye, is a natural part of our physical and mental equipment. All it takes to activate this inner power is the conscious intent to use it.

Traditionally, focusing on the third eye point just above the brows acts like a switch, turning the vision energy inward, energizing areas in the mind, connecting the conscious awareness to inner realities. Just as eyesight provides the perception necessary to operate in the outer world (outer space), triangulating on the third eye opens the mind

to the visions
of
inner space.

In Chapter Three, we used the imagination to take an allegorical trip along the spoke (tunnel) of a Spoke-Focus. There the image of a sparkling crystal gem with the word "imagine" served to illustrate the idea of a journey in, with or through the mind's eye. Here we alter the image slightly to emphasize the idea of imagination as mental creation.

IMAGIN (accent on the first "I") is a little like TRUCKIN'. Think of it as mental truckin.' The word "magi" enclosed between the first and last letters recalls the days of Chaldean magic, Zoroastrian mystics and ancient eastern astrologers. It

is reflected to show that a mage can operate on both sides of the mirror: on the *reflection*, the earth stage and on the *Reflector*, the invisible side of the mobius. As the root word in "imagination" and "image" it implies that the power of imaging is something which transcends the ordinary "flat-plane" view. Notice that the letters in the word "*imagin*" can be spread out to read, "I'm a gin" (in Eastern mythology a "gin" or djinn is a being with magical powers).

The power of *imagin* is subtle and far reaching. In the exercises that follow, the beginner may or may not seem to achieve anything at first, and this doesn't matter. By merely attempting, or *intending* to reach an invisible inner pool of ideas or concepts, the student begins a multifaceted experience that will affect all aspects of her life.

In *imagin*, intent is the tool which accomplishes everything. As you enter into a relaxed state, intend to achieve a triangulation between the two outer eyes and the inner eye, the third eye. With the outer eyes closed, feel the inner eye opening; feel a connection developing. The key word here is "relaxed." Form an image of what you want, hold the thought for a moment, then lightly let it go. Be unconcerned about the results of the exercise.

Traveling to the other side of the mobius requires a light touch. It's a little like visiting a foreign country; you may not know much or any of the language, you may not know how to get around very well, but you come with an interest - you're there to observe, and learn, and enjoy yourself.

In the first set of exercises we will subjectively explore the origins of what THE EXPERIMENT calls the earth Spoke-Focus, the three crossbars of length, width and height that identify the dimensions of space. From there we can move on to the cube, the mobius and beyond. If the exercises seem a little strange to you, don't be deceived. They are powerful, and they lay the groundwork for building the inner spaceship.

The Pythagoreans, who introduced the elements of geometry to the western world, felt that the movements of these elements were the expression of a divine spirit, the Creative Force. Their belief was that all things originated with the MONAD, Indivisible Oneness, which they represented by the geometric element called the Point. Within the MONAD exists all that is possible, the entire potential of the cosmos, but in a latent or unrealized state. It is the extensions of the MONAD into the geometric elements of line, plane and solid that generate the fabric of space and give rise to the concept of duration in space, which is time.

So we mentally recreate these cosmic movements
to lay the groundwork for our journeys through inner space,
as we work, play and explore in THE EXPERIMENT.

CREATING AND EXPLORING THE DIMENSIONS OF SPACE
FROM AN INNER SUBJECTIVE POINT OF VIEW.

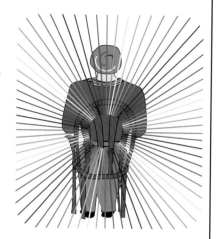

Take a few deep breaths and while inhaling, feel your-self charged with the electrical fiery energy of the air. Hold each breath for a moment while you visualize yourself storing that energy. While exhaling slowly (if you breathe in to the count of three, hold for the same and exhale to the count of six), f-e-e-l the energy flow-ing from a center within, radiating through your body, reaching and touching the infinite. You are a focus of awareness in a matrix of conscious, living energy in which anything is possible.

(Note: if this type of breathing makes you feel lightheaded, lie down to do the exercises.)

With your two eyes closed, turn them upwards to con-tact the third eye, and feel the inner eye being ener-gized by the attention you are placing there. Let this triangulation between the outer and inner lead you into a tranquil, meditative state.

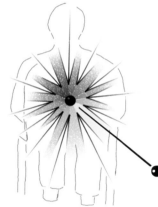

POINT

Imagine the feeling of being reduced to the dimen-sion of a Point. The Point exists in the NO Dimension, at the gateway to space and time. You, as an awareness, are complete, with or without your body. Let go of the feeling of having physical exten-sions, arms, legs, etc. and bring your focus to a Point, WITHIN.

You can do this by pulling in your body until every-thing is contained within the point of focus, or you can focus on the point and let everything else go. Use your prediliction, but try to get the feeling of being within a point of focus with no external distractions.

LINE

While keeping your awareness seated within the Point, imagine a second point existing at any angle or degree of focus somewhere outside of the First Point and feel the connecting line between the two points. This re-enacts the first extension of the Monad into form and establishes the First Dimension, **length**.

You are still you at the first point, as well as at every point along the Line. Imagine the feeling of being extended throughout this Line or of moving back and forth in both directions.

Remember, a Line is infinitely thin: so pull in the loose edges and be truly One-Dimensional.

PLANE

With your awareness extended throughout the line, stretch your focus to a point not on the line.

The extension of your awareness into this point creates the experience of **width**, a triangle, the Second Dimension.

Experience the area of the flat plane within the triangle by feeling the angles and the boundary lines. Then let your awareness extend beyond the boundaries of the triangle to experience the fullest possible range of the Plane. Imagine being extended in every direction throughout an infinitely wide and flat surface,
   the Second Dimension.

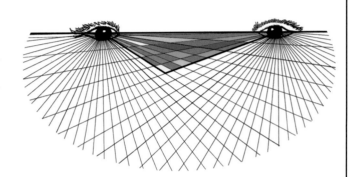

SOLID

Anchor your awareness on the three points of the triangle and then select a fourth point somewhere above the plane of the triangle.

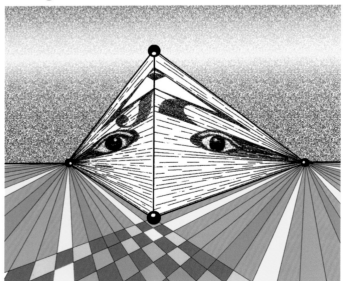

Extend your awareness to encompass this point, and feel yourself expand to fill the space within these four points.

By adding the fourth point, you are mentally creating the experience of **height**,
   the Third Dimension.

After working with the exercises relax and gradually return your focus to its normal state of awareness.

CREATING AND EXPERIENCING THE CUBE, THE INNER SPACESHIP FROM AN INNER SUBJECTIVE POINT OF VIEW.

Relax and triangulate on the third eye by breathing and focusing your intent. Let the two eyes turn upward to contact and awaken the third eye. Pull the vision energy back from the outer world of objects and imagine yourself at a Point, the center of a cube. The three axes of length, width and height that define three-dimensional space originate within you and extend beyond you. See and feel these lines of energy pulsing from the center and reaching out above and below, side to side, in front and behind. Try to see them all simultaneously. (The names we use for the directions, ie. "in front," "behind," originate from the perspective of a consciousness seated in a body that is oriented, because of eyesight, in a forward direction.) By seeing all the energy lines simultaneously, especially the one "behind" us, we begin to break down those limitations of habit and definition. Having said that, be aware that as you loosen your focus from the physical plane and move it into other, invisible ones, you still have a body. Don Juan talks about "the other," the "double," as being an exact duplicate of the physical body - just not limited by time or space.

The cube you create with your imagin will be your inner spaceship and as a ship or plane or spaceship contains you and protects you, so does the inner spaceship. Spend some time in the ship getting familiar with its shape, its proportions. Wherever you travel, you will be within the ship. Build it well and it will always be there for you. The size of the ship is important for it is matched to the size of your body. Imagine yourself standing upright. Your feet will be at the center of the bottom face and your head will touch the center of the top face. Stretch out your arms - your fingertips touch the faces to either side (remember that your outstretched arms equal your height so this gives you a good way to gauge the size). Find the center-point of your body. (Carlos Castaneda mentions in one of his books that don Juan had him measure himself hundreds of times to find his exact centerpoint.) It is an important point, physically and energetically. All lines of travel originate here and return here. Your awareness will be seated here.

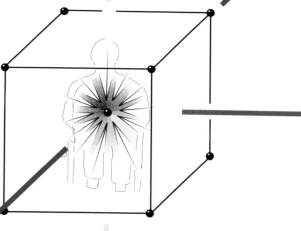

From this point you will "see" in any direction without turning, or in all directions simultaneously.

From your center point awareness, choose a line and travel along it, up or down, right or left, forward or backward. Feel your cube spaceship sliding along each line. Note the subjective differences between each direction.

Next, extend your perception along all six directions simultaneously and feel your consciousness expanding to fill the Cosmos. Then draw your perception in, back to the point and keep going in - explore the world within the point.

❖   ❖   ❖

After each extension return your awareness to experience the center point of origin. When you are finished, return to your inner space, and then to normal consciousness but keep the awareness of your journey with you.

SOME NOTES ON TRAVELING

As consciousness units within a body, we are habituated to perceiving the things that lie within the range of our vision. For instance, if a sound behind us catches our attention, we turn around to see what it is. This habit of considering what's behind us as a blank, hidden unknown is a part of the artificial division that we maintain between the visible and invisible aspects of our experience. When working on the inner planes, we have a tendency to take this habit with us - to experience the inner, limitless as though we were in a physical body.

There is a simple "warm-up" that helps get beyond this habit. Close your eyes and imagine yourself looking at something familiar. "See" it in your mind's eye as though your eyes were open and you were looking at it. In the next part, feel the triangulation between your two outer eyes and the inner, third eye. Then locate the fourth point behind the triangle of the three eyes, toward the back of the head, and draw the image backward so that you are seeing the familiar image at the fourth point, behind the eyes. This area at the back of the head is the vision center so you should have no difficulty in forming the image there.

One aspect of this exercise is that it helps you feel the energy beam that flows out through the eyes and focuses on the objects in sight. As you pull the image you have chosen toward the back of the head, you are reversing the beam. You can actually feel the flow of energy slow down and then stop once the image is behind the plane of the eyes. Shifting the perception towards the back of the head is a little like "weighing the anchor" prior to setting out on a voyage because it disconnects the perception from its fixation on the outer world. Try this a few times. Practice feeling the beam. Get used to "seeing" something that is behind your eyes.

Now that we have covered the basics of building the cube, try using it to go somewhere - an inner journey. Begin always by doing some breathing because this energizes the parts of the brain that are active in *imagin*. We recommend that you purchase a book called <u>The Science of Breath</u> by Yogi Ramacharaka. It is a brief but invaluable aid in learning correct breathing techniques. It is listed in the Bibliography at the end of the book.

In the beginning, run briefly through the Point, Line, Plane and Solid movements before visualizing yourself at the center of the Cube, your inner spaceship. Your awareness will always be seated at the centerpoint. Remember that there are infinities of other centerpoints in every direction around you and that all centers of awareness originate from the One Centerpoint that is the All. From your personal point of awareness, send your goodwill, or your blessings, out in every direction. Feel the Love that pulses through the connections that link us.

At first, choose an inner journey that is emotionally neutral. Focus on the mechanics of traveling without looking into something about which you care deeply. Try exploring locations that are familiar to you on the outer layers. Seat yourself at the center of your ship and imagine being at the chosen location. Try not to "look" with the inner eye but relax and let the images develop. Sometimes you'll get thoughts or words instead of images. Remain detached by keeping the energy beam pulled back.

Chapter Three, <u>Consciousness is a Constant</u> began by describing how the same energy could appear differently when perceived from a different angle or degree of focus. Here is the proof of it. As you cruise the locations that are familiar at the outer level, you will see how the energy that appears as one thing at the outer level can appear very differently when perceived from an inner level.

When finished, always return to your centerpoint awareness and let your attention return to normal outer consciousness. Stretch a bit, relax, and perhaps jot down a few notes on where you have been and what you've seen.

◆　　　　　◆　　　　　◆

Ketherin and Corvus were great travelers, and they often traveled together to places that were familiar on this side to see what they looked like from the other side, from inner space. On one occasion, they visited, in their personal inner spaceships, a certain loading dock in an industrial part of town that they knew from their business dealings.

They each went to their personal meditation space to prepare.

◆　　　　　◆　　　　　◆

When first beginning to explore inner space, certain preparations are helpful. A great deal of the preliminary steps involve preparing the take-off area and charging the inner spaceship with energy. We mentioned, above, the exercise of drawing the energy beam of vision backwards from its normal projection into the world of objects. The beam will energize anything, so when you reverse it, it energizes the area behind the eyes and this is the area in which inner space travel occurs.

Breathing is vitally important. Certain breathing techniques focus on drawing the fiery, electrically-charged energy from the air, the *prana*, and using it to energize a chosen area. Using these techniques in preparing for travel is analogous to fueling up the ship. As you breathe, pull the energy beam toward the back of the head and direct the breath energy to focus on and charge the point at the center of the cube, your inner spaceship.

Feel yourself at the center point and release the feeling of having a physical body. One way to accomplish this is to feel your body being pulled to the centerpoint so that all is contained within the point of vibrating, charged energy which forms the center of the cube. Feel your consciousness seated at that point, and see the crossbars, red, yellow and blue extending from that center.

At this point, your personal style will determine how you travel. Some will zip off in the ship, going here and there, exploring territories known and unknown. Others will simply center their consciousness within the ship and let their *intent* bring a scene before their perception without feeling that they have moved at all.

◆   ◆   ◆

Back to our travelers. After making their preparations, each one in their private meditation rooms, they each directed their intent to the loading dock, the location they had chosen to explore. As they kept their awareness focused at the center of their ships, a scene began to develop. Corvus found himself high on a steep mountain path, overlooking a lush, green valley. The mountain side around him was rough and rocky, but everywhere overgrown with shrubs and ferns and trees. Somewhere nearby, a mountain stream crashed through the rocks and boulders to the valley floor far below.

Corvus, whose awareness was watching the scene, noticed that although he felt that the person on the path was himself, he was aware that it was also a young boy. The boy, whose name was Jeremy, was on his way to a small town down in the valley that he could see from his vantage point on the mountain side. Farther down the mountain, also on the path, were several small groups of travelers, some with donkeys loaded with packs. They all seemed to be headed toward the town.

Ketherin, in her ship, focusing on the loading dock in the industrial part of town, also ended up on that same mountain side, overlooking the town. She too, was journeying toward the town. Unlike Corvus, she knew at once where they were, for she had seen this place before, in her dreams and in her meditations. This was the land of *noname*, a parallel reality in which the adventures of Carolyn and Jeremy seemed to reflect events in the lives of Corvus and Ketherin. Or perhaps it was the other way around. It is often said that the dreamer dreams us into being and it may be that the dream is the reality and "reality" the dream.

The teachers in the Experiment advised our travelers to return often to *noname*, and over the years their travels there developed into a story of their adventures "in the service of the King."

◆   ◆   ◆

This was one small journey in inner space. The uses of inner space travel are endless and the individual's prediliction will be her guide. One person might travel to an inner space where her deepest desire is fulfilled. She could bring that experience back to enrich her present and stimulate activity that takes her more quickly to that goal. Another might travel for information, or for entertainment, but whatever one's purpose, the act of creating and using the inner spaceship sharpens the mind, deepens the awareness and opens a channel that links the two sides of ourselves. This link puts the self conscious awareness that deals with the physical world in touch with the part of ourselves that has an awareness of the ALL, and a conversation develops that brings the larger knowledge into our daily lives as it is needed.

Happy trails!

This primer is to introduce various concepts.
Many are in sets of three to triangulate with mentally.
We are giving concepts to your inner mental computer,
points to construct accurate inner definitions
of your reality and its place
on the Spoke-Focus of Consciousness.
With new definitions in place,
we begin the process of TRIANGULATING,
and formulating paths of travel,
explorations based on these new starting points.

Any three points
will give you a variable, a fourth.
Three is the number
that leads to any and all
fourth points.

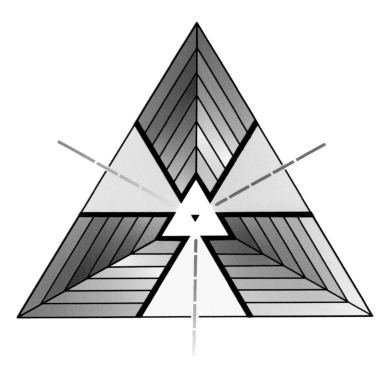

That will end today's session. Our love and guidance is with you at all times.

PART THREE

<u>MINDEXPANDING</u>

CRYSTAL SPRING

A soggy, sad beginning
To a spring that promises fruit
    if the snow will relent
    And melt in the sun's warm caress.
        "Wait!" the Angel of the Crystal cries aloud.
          "Not yet, not yet.
            Let me make the perfect form.
            Each one bespeaks the Name anew.
        Let me harden and create
        Yet another star.
            Let me lay atop the earth
            And spell the curves and folds
                Of her soft skin.
                Let me, as a crystal
                  Seep gently into water
                  To trickle in the runnels
                  Of her streams."

Spring,
　Earth's daughter
Wavers not
　She heeds not the angel's cry,
　　Rather laughs and quickly warms the forms
　　That struggle to maintain a life too late
　　In the cycle's inevitable turn.
　　　"Cry on, . . . battle,
　　　Do as thou will!"
　　　Laughs the Angel of Water.
　"Radiant, hard and strictly shaped,
　Or soft on petals newly awake,
　It matters not, for either way
　I Am the Robe That Wears the Day."

135

CHAPTER SEVEN
CRYSTALS & MINERALS

July 2, 1980

This morning I was sitting in the study of Corvus, my partner. The sun was shining brightly and I watched the rainbow lights dancing on the walls from the cut glass crystals blowing in the open window. The rays of light intersecting the moving, multifaceted surfaces were being refracted into a thousand dancing bursts of color. . .KM.

A crystal of this type is a good example of a Spoke-Focus; each angled facet that bends or reflects the light coming through it is an angle distortion. The shapes of the leaded glass crystals and their myriad designs of interrelating angles give you an accurate image of the infinite variations within a Spoke-Focus.

The rainbow refractions of the crystals in the sunlight, the dancing, moving, vibrating spectrums are the closest in imagery and definition to the way in which the One Reality, represented by white light, reflects Itself into infinitely variable probable realities, one of which is your three-dimensional earth reality.

The single earth reality that your senses perceive appears relatively static in comparison to the flashing, scintillating Source. However, the earth patterns that you see, the shapes of the earth system, are the visible reflections of ALL THAT IS, and they are there to show you how the system works. The way in which a snowflake forms, the growth of crystals and minerals - these are the earth patterns. These stylized, regular designs, when seen with the use of magnification, illustrate the Intelligence at work in creation. With practice, you may relate the patterns found in the mineral world to ALL THAT IS and begin to see them as part of a living, conscious whole.

CONSIDER how we think about the physical material of the earth. The atomic theory of matter is point oriented. Everything is constructed of points: particles, electrons, protons, neutrons, atoms, atomic elements. These points build up complex forms by joining with other points to amass a physical, visible structure: the mineral world, the earth, the sun, star systems, galaxies, all the material in the known universe.

That is the material point of view, the objective, flat-plane view. In THE EXPERIMENT, this view of the universe as object is called the *reflection* to indicate a view seen in a mirror, implying something larger, "more real," outside the immediate view that, through the medium of reflection, is taking on shape in three dimensions.

OBJECTIVE
proceeding from the object, known

SUBJECTIVE
proceeding from the subject, knowing

The objective view describes external forces acting at random, controlling every physical interaction in the universe, blindly developing form, life and even consciousness, through a series of accidental, or random combinations. Each of the myriad objects in this scenario is thought to be independent, separate, distinct. The subjective view, on the other hand, sees each individual form, whether atom, crystal, star or human being, as an extension, in three dimensions, of the universal life energy, ALL THAT IS. There is no separate existence because every manifestation, every appearance derives its being from the unified Oneness variously known as the SOURCE, ALL THAT IS, the ABSOLUTE. In THE EXPERIMENT, this view is called the *Reflector* to indicate that all-encompassing reality which reflects ITSELF into form, or into our sphere of awareness.

When looking at mineral and crystal patterns, we are seeing the shape of a living system, set in stone, so to speak. This system, the mineral world, is literally the underlying substructure, that which supports us, the ground of our being. What we see in the patterns of the mineral world are clues to the workings of a larger reality that is invisible to two eyes, but visible within, with the third eye.

The ancient Greek philosopher-scientists who introduced the concepts of the shape of space to the western world were grounded in a spiritual interpretation of reality. The mathematical insights of Pythagoras and his followers were considered to be glimpses of a radiant world of Divine Order, the Archetypal Plane of Shape which held the Master Patterns or templates for all earthly form.

Their vision of the shape of space, the four-point matrix we explored subjectively in the last chapter, is the framework upon which physical reality is built, the gateway through which energy passes in order to become visible in three dimensions.

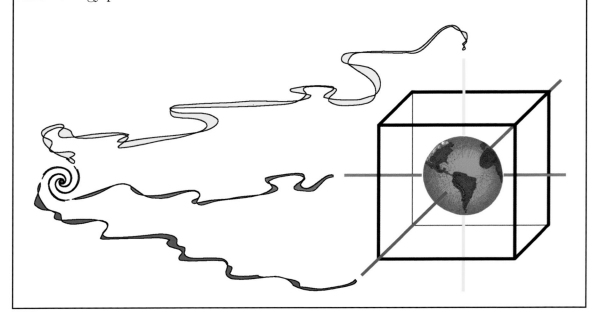

The Pythagorean exploration of shape focused on the "regular" shapes, as these were considered the ideal or pure forms. On the flat plane, two dimensions, there are an infinite number of regular shapes starting with the equilateral triangle (3 sides), the square (four sides), the pentagon (5 sides) on up through hexagons, septagons and octagons with each successive figure more closely approximating the shape of a circle (FIG. 1). In each of these figures, the sides are all of the same length, and the interior angles where the sides meet are identical, hence the term "regular."

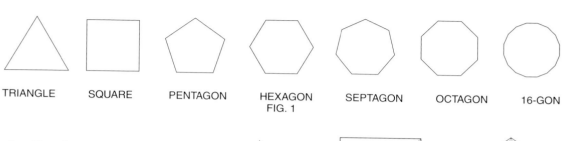

TRIANGLE   SQUARE   PENTAGON   HEXAGON   SEPTAGON   OCTAGON   16-GON
FIG. 1

In the first three regular figures in two-dimensional space, Pythagoreans found ratios that reveal mathematical laws, acoustical harmonics and patterns for crystalline growth as well as proportions that govern harmony in nature, art and architecture.

DIVISION OF THE EQUILATERAL TRIANGLE YIELDS THE 30°- 60°- 90° RIGHT TRIANGLE ($A^2+B^2= C^2$).

DIVISION OF THE SQUARE YIELDS THE 45°- 45°- 90° RIGHT TRIANGLE, WITH THE RATIO OF $1 : 1 :\sqrt{2}$

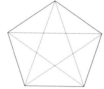

THE PROPORTIONS REVEALED BY THE DIVISION OF THE PENTAGON ARE SO FAR-REACHING THEY ARE CALLED THE "GOLDEN SECTION," OR THE DIVINE PROPORTION.

Pythagorean thought on shape and proportion went far beyond the faculties of reason alone; their meditations brought them into contact with Cosmic Consciousness, the World Shaper. In an attempt to communicate the truths of that contact, they derived a symbolic explanation: that as the energy of creation comes into three dimensions, it is shaped by the angles and triangles found in the figures illustrated above. The essence of these shapes and the proportions they embody are the true origin of all *form* in three dimensions. Though this may sound quaint or obscure to the "modern mind," one has only to examine the shape of a snowflake to begin to see what the ancient philosophers were trying to express.

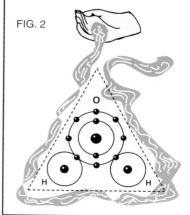

FIG. 2

SNOWFLAKE PATTERNS

Snowflakes all take their shape from the three-way pattern that occurs when two hydrogen atoms combine with one oxygen atom to make water (FIG. 2).

Snowflakes crystallize directly from the invisible atoms in the atmosphere, each producing one of an infinite number of variations that can form around the basic triangular shape of H_2O (FIG 3).

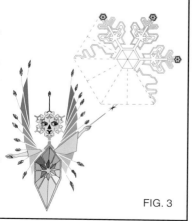

FIG. 3

PLATONIC SOLIDS

When the Pythagoreans began using the flat-plane shapes to build three-dimensional solids, they found that there are only five shapes in the entire manifested universe that can form as "regular" solids, figures having all equal faces, lines and angles. These figures only occur when a set of regular two-dimensional figures fits together perfectly to enclose a volume of space (FIG. 1). This was a timeless, monumental discovery, for it meant that these five simple shapes were the template for all three-dimensional form.

To the ancient Greeks, four of the solids represented the four elements, and the fifth, the dodecahedron, was thought to be the Quintessence - the Consciousness of the Cosmos. But beyond the attributions, Pythagoreans felt that in these shapes, they held the key to the mysteries of three-dimensional existence, and, as always, their ideas have turned out to be startlingly accurate, for the Platonic Solids describe precisely the molecular shape of the earth's mineral structure.

FIG. 1

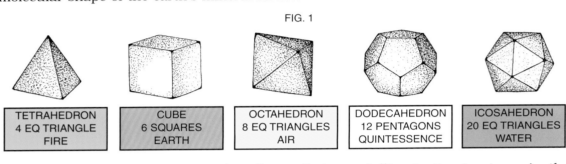

| TETRAHEDRON 4 EQ TRIANGLE FIRE | CUBE 6 SQUARES EARTH | OCTAHEDRON 8 EQ TRIANGLES AIR | DODECAHEDRON 12 PENTAGONS QUINTESSENCE | ICOSAHEDRON 20 EQ TRIANGLES WATER |

All of the solid, inorganic material in the earth is crystalline in its structure. As the molten material at the center of the earth moves toward the surface in liquid form, it cools, and the atoms slow down enough to begin combining in stabilized patterns. At this point, the elements come together in beautifully-ordered crystalline lattices that form the atomic sub-structure of every mineral substance in the earth's crust.

To use a common example, when atoms of sodium and chlorine combine as salt they form in a cubic shaped lattice defined by three equal lines with 90° angles between them (FIG. 2).

Sodium and chlorine atoms alternate along the lines, and each atom is the center of another set of lines so that the lattice pattern in FIG. 3 extends throughout the entire crystalline mass.

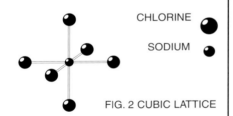

CHLORINE

SODIUM

FIG. 2 CUBIC LATTICE

This lattice pattern is invisible to the naked eye, but when enough atoms accumulate to make visible salt crystals, they form, not surprisingly, as tiny cubes.

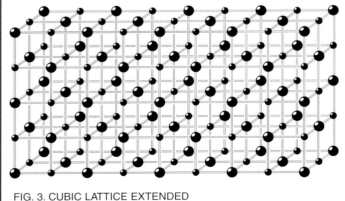

FIG. 3. CUBIC LATTICE EXTENDED

SALT CRYSTALS

We use salt as an example since it is a common mineral that crystallizes in a shape that perfectly reflects the shape of the underlying atomic structure. Every mineral has an atomic lattice structure: there are fourteen different lattice patterns in which atoms can combine and seven crystal systems that classify the different patterns. Most all, however, are variations on the cubic structure seen in salt, the three-crossbar shape that in THE EXPERIMENT is called the basic earth Spoke-Focus, three equal and mutually perpendicular axes (x-y-z).

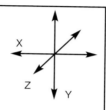

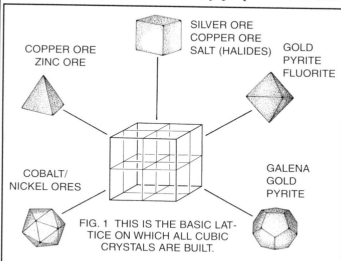

COPPER ORE
ZINC ORE

SILVER ORE
COPPER ORE
SALT (HALIDES)

GOLD
PYRITE
FLUORITE

COBALT/
NICKEL ORES

GALENA
GOLD
PYRITE

FIG. 1 THIS IS THE BASIC LATTICE ON WHICH ALL CUBIC CRYSTALS ARE BUILT.

This shape, which describes three-dimensional space, also describes the ideal shapes in space, the Platonic Solids. Each of the five Solids is a cubic structure - obvious with the cube and octahedron, but a close look at the others will show that they all form around the same Spoke-Focus shape as the cube. And the minerals of the cubic system of crystals (first of the seven crystal systems) stand out for one principal reason - they often form crystals in the shapes of the Platonic Solids.

When the conditions are right for crystallization, atoms that fit into this structure drop into position, filling up the lattice to create specific minerals, depending upon the combination of elements present. Salt (previous page) forms when a sodium atom occupies the center of the cube and chlorine atoms fill the center of each face.

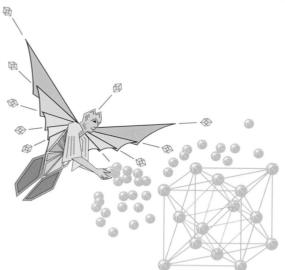

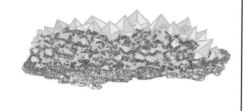

Gold forms when atoms of gold drop into position at each corner of the cubic lattice and at the center of each face. Sometimes the shape of the mineral is a perfect crystal solid; more often it is distorted or unrecognizable, but the underlying lattice always maintains the exact geometric relationship between atoms.

That the Solids exist as a type of Master Pattern for the shape of reality is remarkable, but that the earth produces lumps of rock in those shapes is miraculous. It is a true justification of Pythagorean thought that the Master Shaper works through the principles of Geometry.

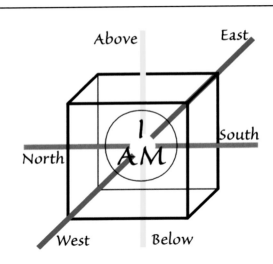

Pythagoreans and others have gone beyond using the Spoke-Focus shape to describe just the material objects around us. They also use it to describe our selves as consciousness units functioning in three dimensions.

Each subjective consciousness (the Self), is seen as a centerpoint of focus in relation to the six directions of space. Thus each unit functions as a seven-fold construct.

And just as each atom in a crystal lattice is connected to every other atom throughout the crystalline mass, we, as centerpoints of focus, are connected to every point in the Spoke-Focus of consciousness, throughout our local aspect of reality and beyond.

According to the tradition of Wisdom that comes down through the ages, each consciousness unit is both a receiving station and a transmitting station. We receive influences from every direction of the Cosmos, including influences from past and future events. And we transmit our reactions to these influences (the thoughts we energize, the words we speak) out into the ether to reach and communicate instantaneously with the farthest reaches of the Cosmos, past, present and future. Incidentally, this is not a view that is limited to Ageless Wisdom - it is supported by aspects of modern theoretical physics.

In modern science, the concept of the central observer, or Self, is coming out from behind the veil of esotericism, as it is crucial to an understanding of Relativity and quantum mechanics. These pictures of reality only make sense from the viewpoint of a central consciousness. The Observer is the key factor in Einstein's thought experiments and in the interpretation of quantum effects. It is the element that is taking science from the realm of the objective (the object being known) into the realm of the subjective (the Subject, knowing). As Einstein pointed out, any interpretation of an event depends upon the position of the Individual in relation to the surrounding space(time), an idea that was also of the greatest importance to Pythagoreans in their quest to understand our place in the universe.

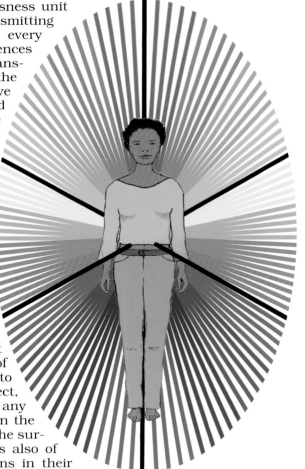

Perhaps the Pythagoreans were not aware that the shapes of the Solids were mirrored in the atomic crystal lattices of all the minerals, but being scientist-seers of the highest order, perhaps they were. After all, the Greeks introduced the idea of the atom, and the Pythagoreans insisted that all material form derived from the patterns found in the Solids.

Consider their teachings regarding the Tetrahedron, the geometric solid created by four points. It is the first Platonic Solid and the simplest shape that can exist in three dimensions and therefore it represents the origin of form. The four triangular faces of the Tetrahedron were seen as the four elements, and its centerpoint represented the fifth element, the Quintessence: Consciousness, the Creator and Observer of the manifested world.

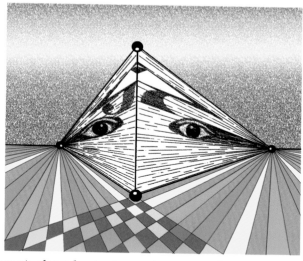

Now consider how this abstract mathematical-metaphysical concept describes the actual form or shape of the mineral world. There are thousands of known minerals in the fourteen lattices of the seven crystal systems, but beneath the classified lattice structures, two of the most abundant elements on earth, Silica and Oxygen, combine geometrically in the shape of a regular tetrahedron (FIG. 1) to make up the basic elemental substructure of *over 90% of the solid material in the earth's crust.*

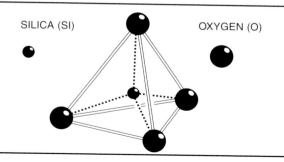

FIG. 1. **THE SILICA-OXYGEN TETRAHEDRON**
A SYMBOL OF CONSCIOUSNESS
EXTENDED INTO LIVING FORM.
OXYGEN, THE BREATH OF LIFE,
AT THE FOUR CORNERS
AND AT THE CENTER, **SILICA**,
THE MINERAL WE USE IN CREATING
(ARTIFICIAL) INTELLIGENCE.

SILICA (SI)   OXYGEN (O)

the interconnectedness of all things in relation to the attributions of the Tetrahedron. Pythagoreans named it the element of fire. One interpretation might be that when a tetrahedron rests on its base, it always points upward, like a flame. Perhaps so. But examine the names of the elements that make up the silica - oxygen tetrahedron and a deeper meaning emerges. The root of "silica" is the Latin word, **silex** - flint. Flint is the material used to strike a fire. Oxygen is the element that feeds fire. One of the origins of the word "oxygen" is from the Greek word **gignesthai** - to be born.

Thus the Tetrahedron (the manifested universe) can be seen as that which is born of fire. Compare this with our current scientific notion that the Big Bang, a fireball of intense magnitude, is the origin of the entire manifested universe. These are not accidental relationships - everything is related at levels that reach through time and space to connect us with ALL THAT IS.

ANGLE DISTORTION

All the mineral and crystal patterns that we have been examining are reflections, and they come into existence through angle distortion.

> ANGLE
> [SKR. anka - HOOK]
> hook; bend; change of direction;
> standpoint, or point of view.
>
> DISTORTION
> [L. dis - APART + **torqueo** - TWIST]
> a twisting apart.

Think back to Chapter Three, where you saw that the way light is refracted (bent, or deflected) is the way the mathematically-proportioned angle distortions of earth's focus create appearances, materializations.

When the invisible energy of the Boundless passes through the mirror of earth perception, IT reflects ITSELF into visible form. The bend, or change of direction, is a shift in the point of view, from the *Reflector*, where all is possible, to the *reflection*, the specific manifestation. Angle distortion involves a twisting apart, a separation whereby the *Reflector becomes* the *reflection*. That is why it is angle distortion, **dis-torqueo**, an appearance of separateness, just as your reflection in a mirror produces a separate appearance of yourself, the subject seemingly reversed into object.

The *Reflector* sends out an image, the *reflected*,
and seems to separate from Itself, and form a new "Itself,"
a reflection of Itself,

ITS IMAGE REVERSED

These reflections are located *at angles, at every degree*, in all patterns. As each snowflake is unique, so each variable of angle dis-torsion is possible in the patterns visible to you in the mineral kingdom.

There is a mathematical probable for every crystal shape possible. Therefore there is a visible reflection of ALL THAT IS, in all the ways in which these probables interrelate. When you see the reflections of these patterns on earth, you see them represented as if on a flat plane.

Remember that this is an illusion.

Actually,
ALL SPACE IS CURVED; ALL MOTION IS SPIRAL.

The idea of curved space is one that has come into general acceptance with Einstein's Theory of Relativity. In his vision of reality, the gravity associated with massive bodies (stars, planets, etc.) has the effect of curving the fabric of space-time. Due to the laws of momentum, a planet always moves ahead in a "straight" line but it does so in a curved space; the result is its orbital path around the sun. A ship on the ocean may plot a course that takes it straight ahead by the compass, but since it travels on a curved surface, its forward motion describes an arc. A planet moves through the curved space around the sun in an unvarying elliptical orbit and it appears to be passing through the same space year after year. However, if space-time is a single fabric, then the planet's orbit is really a spiral - it never crosses the same space-time because it moves through time while it is travelling through space (FIG. 1).

Satellite images show the spiral motion of hurricanes and the whirling track of storms moving across the surface of the earth. Closer to home, we can see how leaves in the wind spiral and whirl, how water in a stream flows in whorls and vortices. Branches grow in spirals around the trunks of trees, roots grow in spirals in the earth, flowers and seeds form in spiral patterns. Whirling motion is the primary pattern of reality, visible in all things.

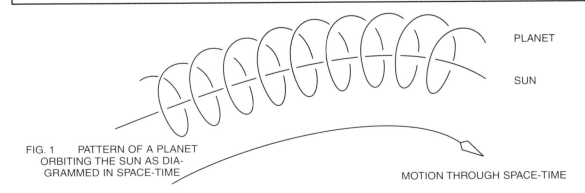

PLANET

SUN

FIG. 1   PATTERN OF A PLANET
ORBITING THE SUN AS DIA-
GRAMMED IN SPACE-TIME

MOTION THROUGH SPACE-TIME

The patterns of reality's building blocks are described most clearly, in the language of Basic, through the mineral kingdom. These patterns show you the flat-plane view, the way you perceive the reflection. You may, however, translate the flat-plane view into the *Reflector* view by applying the Law.

In looking at mineral and crystal patterns, remember that the pattern is the *reflection*. The *Reflector* is the Source. IT reflects ITSELF into three-dimensional form as a mineral or a crystal.

Snowflakes, crystalline mineral structures, show you the patterns of specific earth appearances. You may then place the patterns correctly, on a curve, and re-evaluate them, knowing that they are on a curve, a spiral; one of many possibles, all interacting. No longer is it just a snowflake, or a crystal; it is *one of infinite number*. Then remember the Law:

THE INFINITE NUMBER
MAKE THE ONE.

By applying THE LAW of looking to the *Reflector* and not at the *reflection*, we make a mental act that aligns us with the Source of power. It is a subtle shift of focus, but one that reverberates through our personal reality and changes our relation to the Cosmos.

THE ALL makes all appearances
of all the seemingly separate ways
THE ALL reflects ITSELF,
through angle distortion.

Its energy rays out,
seems to twist
and then becomes. . .
anything, all things,

itself as infinite number.

Remember Einstein's curve of space-time. The flat-plane earth appearance is so ingrained in our perception that in times past, people thought that the earth was flat. After it was accepted that the earth and other heavenly bodies were spheres, it still seemed reasonable to assume that space was flat. Even now that Einstein's vison is part of our description of reality, it is difficult to grasp in the face of appearances. When we look out into the night sky, it seems that there is a straight line between us and any star we see. We incorporate the flat-plane assumption into our language. We say, "I'm looking straight at it," but the light from the star that seems straight in front of us has travelled through curved space. The fact that we know this doesn't change the way it looks, but it does remind us of the mystery that lies behind the mask of appearances.

The translation, from flat plane to curved is an important mental distinction we are being asked to make. If it seems abstract, try this exercise. Look at a picture, a photograph, a flat-plane representation of a three-dimensional reality. It is static - it conveys but one aspect of the larger multi-dimensional reality it represents. Now imagine yourself in the midst of that scene - bring it alive by hearing the sounds, smelling the smells, feeling the sensations. If it is a woodland scene, feel the breeze, notice that each leaf on every tree is in constant motion. If it's of a waterfall, feel the spray, hear the roar of the water. Whatever the scene in the picture, the reality will be in motion, constantly changing from moment to moment, a rich multivariable experience that could never be expressed by the picture. It is the same with the flat-plane view of reality: much more is going on than meets the eye.

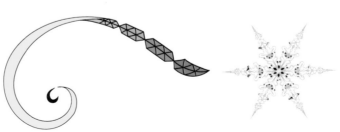

The ten triangles (FIG. 1) and the Qabalistic Tree of Life (FIG. 2) are forms or descriptions in the *language of shape* that can illustrate the larger Law at work. This crystalline-like structure of ten triangles is a living concept, an expression in BASIC, a segment of a continuous multi-dimensional structure, on a curve, a spiral of flat-plane angle distortions (FIG. 3). Each point of the triangles where the lines intersect is a co-ordinate point. (On the Tree of Life it is called a Sphere, a Sephiroth.)

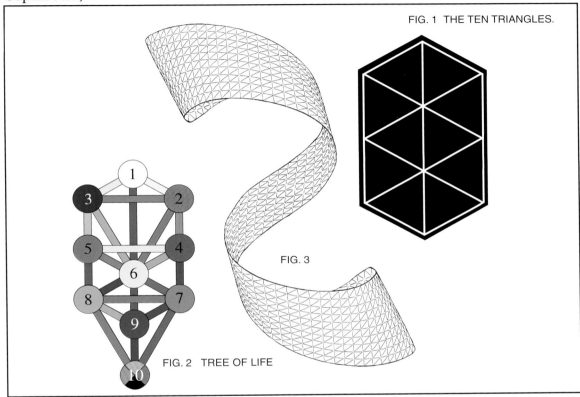

FIG. 1 THE TEN TRIANGLES.

FIG. 3

FIG. 2 TREE OF LIFE

This triangle design is basic to your reality, as you are three-dimensional expressions of ALL THAT IS. Your earth definitions are all in three-point reference. That is why you can easily triangulate and use two points to find a third.

Look at the ten triangle design for a moment. It is, at first glance, a flat-plane drawing of ten equilateral triangles, but with a *shift of the focus*, it can also be seen three-dimensionally, as two cubes. See the diagram as flat-plane triangles then change it into a solid figure. Let the hard and fast focus of the two eyes soften a bit, withdraw the energy beam coming through the eyes and let your intent make the shift. The shift from the two-eye view to using the third eye is as simple and as subtle a shift as that. (See p. *202* for more on the ten triangles and the *four facets of focus*. See also p. *189* for a chart of the ten triangles.)

As you cultivate an awareness of the LAW, the *Reflector*, the invisible reality that surrounds you, and feel the connection that exists between the two eyes and the third eye, your perception of three-dimensional reality is enhanced and deepened by the flow of energy from the fourth dimension.

Let us explore beyond triangulating and consider quadralating, using three points to find a fourth. In triangulating you start from the two points of the two-eye view and reach to make contact with the third eye. In quadralating, you begin by triangulating on the third eye and using that state as a platform to reach toward various fourth points. Two points find a specific third (the third eye), but three points find one of many possible fourths. We expand here beyond the limits of flat-plane specifications to deal with Variables.

> To quadralate, take two points and find a third
> (triangulate on the third eye),
> then locate one of many fourth points.

Consider this in relation to the mechanics involved in flying. The three points of the landing gear triangulate to maintain stability while the plane gets up enough speed to overcome the limitation of gravity, ie. to move from the second dimension, the runway, into the third dimension, the air. The probable destination(s) is the variable fourth point.

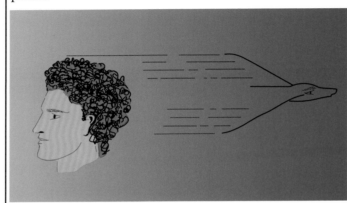

Triangulating on the third eye allows perception to shift into a meditative state where it is highly receptive to knowledge and imagery from beyond the limits of time and space. From that stance it is possible to quadralate on various fourth points and to experience probable, or variable, realities. As the plane gives the body mobility in the third dimension, quadralating is a vehicle for perception to travel into and explore the fourth dimension.

Once the perception has attained an awareness of the fourth point, the original three points become variable. Finding the fourth point frees the first three and gives them a point to center on, to travel, expand and explore their own possible variations.

This applies to mathematical formulas and to life as well.
We have changed a focus point and, in relocating it, become freer.

Keep in mind that the concepts in this primer are not as difficult as they first appear. In a sense they are kept at their most simple. If anything, you must 'simplify' to understand them. To speak the language of Basic you must have a clear, simple set of accurate, working definitions.

Scientific inquiry into the laws of the mineral, crystalline world, as seen in flat-plane imagery, will show the viewer with two eyes the structures of earth reality.

> *Use three eyes, triangulate to see 'the magic',*
> *find the 'fourth point' on the inner planes*
> *and go on from there.*

WALKING THE MOBIUS

A SUBJECTIVE EXPERIENCE
ON AN INNER PLANE

After triangulating on the third eye, pull your attention back to the imaging center at the back of your head. Imagine yourself standing on a flat strip suspended in space. The strip has been twisted into a mobius, but a special gravity holds you perpendicular to the surface at all times, even when the strip is "sideways" or "upside down."

For descriptive purposes we assume that you begin the exercise in the position shown in the illustration. Once you are familiar with the twists and turns of the mobius, you can take the journey anyway you choose.

Feel yourself walking level along the inside of the strip and can see it rising up and twisting overhead to connect with the path behind you. As you walk "up" the first rise you will be upside down, then you encounter the twist - you are now moving forward and sideways at the same time, moving from the inside to the outside of the strip. Ahead the strip curves to the left. You are still sideways and as you follow the path, you end up on the underside of the strip. You have made one complete revolution, but instead of being at the starting point, you are upside down, below the starting point. You may feel the same (right is still right and left is left), but because of the twist, to an outside observer you appear not only upside down but also reversed side to side.

Now you will make another full circuit, but on the other side of the strip. Subjectively experience the differences of each feature of the mobius from the other side. From an upside down position below the starting point, proceed around the curve of the path heading up over the top and then sideways, through the twist and around the inside curve to end up at the starting point. Subjectively experience the truly unique feeling of moving forward while your "body" is sideways. Resist the overwhelming temptation to create the normal feeling of walking on earth. After a few times around, try to feel your identical double walking the other side of the mobius, step for step, a mobius reflection of yourself. When you are finished with the exercise, return to your calm state of triangulation, and then back to normal awareness.

Feel both sides.

A WAKING DREAM

Our traveler is on a journey of discovery, seeking to understand some aspect of the inner reality behind the outer appearances of three-dimensional existence. She has triangulated on her third eye point and found the stillness that comes from turning within.

After centering her attention at the back of the head, she works with the cube exercise to develop an awareness of her extensions and to acquire a flexible and fluid focus. She is curious to know why the ancients taught that understanding the cube can open the mind to hidden worlds.

She explores the direction Within, and as she floats in the stillness at the center of the cube, she slowly becomes conscious of a curving, spiralling, moving strip extending infinitely. Drawn by the sight, she moves closer and sees that the strip is a portion of the mobius, covered with a grid of sparkling waving lines of light.

As her perception adjusts, she sees that the strip appears to be a grid of triangles and then remembers having asked to be shown something about the curve of three-dimensional space-time.

Walking on the strip as in the mobius exercises, she begins to notice that what first looked like a triangle grid on the surface of the strip is also something more. It was only the habit pattern of seeing the flat-plane view that had made it seem flat. Now, with a start, she sees that she is climbing on a grid of cubes and thinks of the lattice shape at the heart of all cubic crystals.

The thought occurs to her that if the Platonic Solids represent the ideal of shape in three-dimensional space and if they all form around this cubic lattice (FIG 1), then the essence of three-dimensional time-space earth reality is defined by this shape: the earth Spoke-Focus.

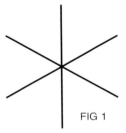

FIG 1

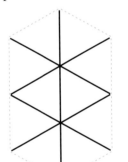

FIG 2

The single Spoke-Focus represents earth, three dimensions, solidity, the cube. The ten triangle/double cube design that she sees in the grid at her feet is formed by a double Spoke-Focus shape (FIG 2). She knows that a flat-plane grid of regular triangles has been used from the most ancient of times as a symbol representing the matrix of creation. The doubling of the earth Spoke-Focus represents a movement from the single earth reality, the world of appearances where a lamppost is always a lamppost, into the magical realm of the double, a state beyond the limitations of space and time.

With this realization our traveler sees that a simple shift of her focus can change the scene before her back and forth from a grid of three-dimensional cubes one moment to a grid of flat-plane triangles the next. As she alternates between the view of triangles and then cubes, then triangles, she understands that she can move, at will, between the flat-plane view, the *reflection*, and the *Reflector* view which is constantly moving, changing and variating.

As the vision begins to fade, the traveller returns to her inner space, the stillness within, and then slowly back to her normal, earth awareness. But she has expanded and grown and takes the lesson of her journey with her. She no longer accepts the earth appearance at face value. She feels the largeness around her and knows that existence pulses between visible (the *reflection*) and invisible (the *Reflector*).

She has changed her focus point, and in relocating it, become freer.

TURNINGS

When on lonely mountain peaks
I reach within
To the eye of the hurricane
I am encouraged,
I am welcomed.

The whirling spirals spin me dry
Until, like dust,
I am carried away
To scatter
On the earth's plains.

I become one with the red clay
Of sculpted wealth,
The yellow sand
Introduces the blue waters.

In totality
In All
I am One
With the force
That Whirls.

As we think, so we create.

CHAPTER EIGHT
THE FOURTH POINT

Inquiry into the fourth dimension demands a process of deductive reasoning,
based on facts both visible and invisible.

You must read the visible correctly:

reversed bɘƨɿɘvɘɿ
ɿɘvɘɿƨɘd bɘƨɿɘvɘɿ

as   Mirror   images
       Wiɿɿoɿ

*The invisible may be
deduced by the surrounding
evidence.*

The invisible is visible in the visible world. You must learn to read it correctly. As tire tracks tell of cars that are now invisible to you, so the visible world is filled with the charts and maps of the invisible, *left behind* in your speed zone.

The invisible world is traveling at another speed, another vibration and so is therefore *not seen* per se, but its path can be seen. You can chart the stars by the spaces between. You can learn to look into and between things to see the unseen.

"Rainbow Beemer, definitely."

The fourth point that we are exploring is not defined as are the other three. The fourth point is of the invisible world, not specific and defined as you have been taught to expect in your definitions of REAL.

This non-specific, fluid, fourth point is real, but variable, and therefore your reality tends to dismiss it as imaginary, or make-believe.

You don't have to *make* yourself believe something you define as *not real*. You have only to broaden your definitions of real to include the unseen, the unheard, the invisible.

X-rays are *real*.

Ultraviolet is *real*.

Sound waves are *real*.

You see, your cultures have advanced to the knowledge that real *does* include the un-seen and the un-heard. Now expand creatively into the UN world and accept the evidence of

INNER knowledge,

INNER evidence.

Define INNER as REAL.

In the blending of the world's people, you can incorporate the knowledge of inner reality that comes from the East with the process of scientific inquiry that comes from the West.

Combine these and enter into the 21st Century, the New Age, with a whole unexplored region ahead: Inner Realities, the fourth dimension(s). An "s" is added as the rule applies:

four is variable.

Points 1, 2, and 3 are fixed,

by your present definitions and standards,

but point 4 is flexible

and once we have located it,

then points 1, 2 and 3 become flexible too.

This concept of the flexibility of any one and/or all of the four points is of the utmost importance. We are dealing with living, moving structures of thought, *made solid* in certain vibration zones.

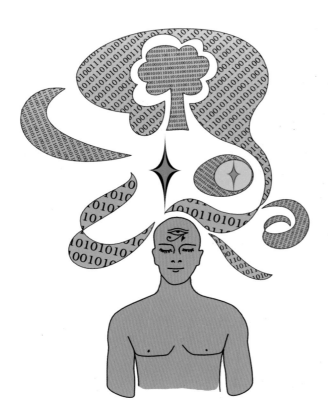

Made solid means only that these thought-structures will APPEAR to be fixed in time-space. In actuality, they are constantly moving, changing, interacting and affecting each other.

As this becomes a premise of your reality, you will begin to see and sense what was once invisible. The new inner computer tapes with the new definitions will help to make the invisible visible.

We accept, in our new premises, the solidity and substance of thought in both the visible and invisible realms. We know that thoughts are manifest in the ether that surrounds us. They are only invisible because they travel at a rate other than that of earth's visible range, yet they do exist, they are real.

Like x-rays and ultraviolet light, thoughts are there, measurable, invisible, not seen with two eyes; yet they may be sensed when one triangulates on the third inner eye.

This creates the fourth.

*The fourth point we seek
is a number-related
point-structure in Time-Space.
It is variable within
the mathematical limits of three.
It may be easily located*
within
by defining invisible as **real***.*

Just as you create a reality
by using your focus,
so you create the third point
by triangulating from two points,
and create the fourth point by
quadralating from three points.
Keep in mind that this description
is a *REFLECTED* view.

The view from the *REFLECTOR*
is the opposite:
the four points
create the three points
which create the two points
which create the one point.

REFLECTED   VIEW

REFLECTOR   VIEW

THE ALL CREATES THE SPECIFIC.

THE MANY CREATE THE FEW.

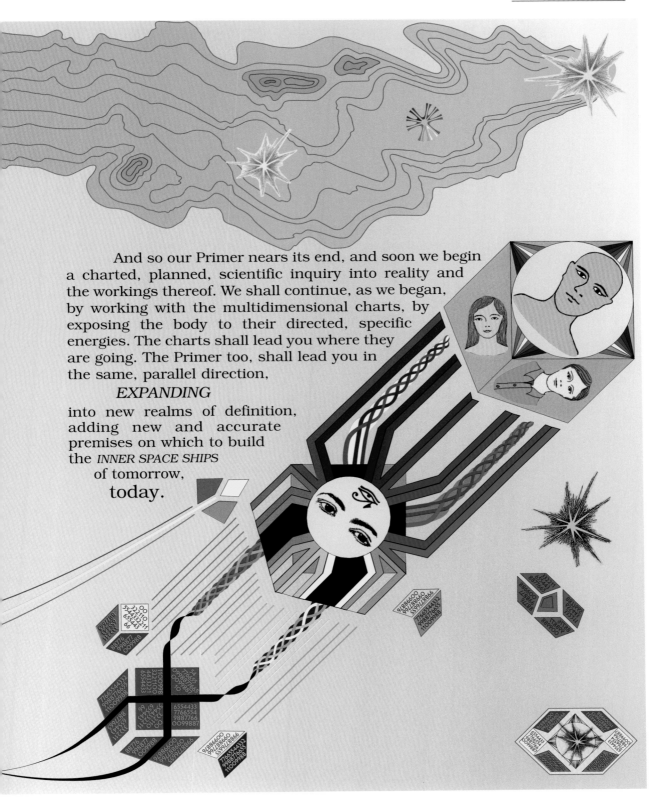

And so our Primer nears its end, and soon we begin a charted, planned, scientific inquiry into reality and the workings thereof. We shall continue, as we began, by working with the multidimensional charts, by exposing the body to their directed, specific energies. The charts shall lead you where they are going. The Primer too, shall lead you in the same, parallel direction,

EXPANDING

into new realms of definition, adding new and accurate premises on which to build the *INNER SPACE SHIPS* of tomorrow,

today.

AN IN-BETWEEN

CONSIDER
CON-WITH SIDER-STARS
WITH STARS CON SIDER

Ideas are the primary reality that precede all physical manifestation. They are the foundation of everything we create, make or do. According to the ancient Greek philosophers of the Platonic tradition, thought and image exist on an archetypal plane of idea - to them a very real place: the origin and source of inspiration for all mortal undertakings.

IDEA
[GR. idea - TO SEE **]**
TO PLATO: AN ARCHETYPE, AN INDEPENDENT UNIVERSE.
TO ARISTOTLE: THE FORM, OR FORM-GIVING CAUSE.

THINK
[L. cogitare - TO HAVE IDEAS, TO REFLECT**]**
to know, to seem or appear, to form in the mind

THOUGHT
the act or process of thinking; mental concentration on ideas as distinguished from sense perceptions or emotions; reflection.

One of the ways we become aware of this plane is in the first, faint glimmering of an idea. At this point, an idea is without shape or form - it is archetypal in nature and infinite in possibility. The creative function of mind takes this hint of an idea and clothes it with related thoughts (depending upon one's subjective focus or point of view) and so begins to shape it. The formative function fully shapes the idea so that it exists completely on a mental plane, almost solid. Then, by the action of physical processes, it is brought into the material world.

We commonly accept something as "real" once it appears in solid form, and yet the reality of the thing in question is present at all stages from before our first awareness of it in the world of thought to its appearance in three dimensions. It has long been known in Hermetic philosophy, and more recently re-discovered in medical and psychiatric research, that repeated thoughts tend to manifest as three-dimensional actualities.

"...for thoughts are deeds...what one thinks continually they become; what one cherishes in their heart and mind they make a part of the pulsation of their heart...and build in their own physical."
Edgar Cayce

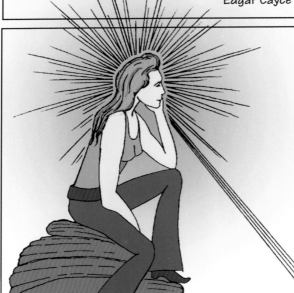

"My thoughts and I are of another world."
Ben Jonson

Thought shapes and creates reality. If this appears subjective, remember that since Einstein and the quantum revolution there is no "objective" world out there: the world is as we each define it. Our perception of reality is subjective, but as our knowledge grows, our definitions change. Consider the Fifteenth Century, when we collectively began to redefine reality from earth-centered to sun-centered.

The Pythagoreans, forerunners of modern science, subscribed to the idea that the universe is MIND and that the product of MIND, thought, is the substance which is the essence of matter. Science tells us that the one essential substance in the universe is light, and throughout the ages teachers have asserted that this substance is a conscious Intelligence.

The Pythagoreans called this the Quintessence, the force of thought, or Intelligence.

As we think, so we create.

When we quadralate we enter the world of thought, free from the limitations of three-dimensional existence. Remember that thought is a substance which you can use to create and build, just as are bricks and mortar. There are differences. In the material world, the body acts very deliberately, placing each brick in a predetermined position; in mental creation, one simply holds the seed thought in mind and lets the related thoughts gather spontaneously. Cultivate a "hands off" attitude and watch.

Begin by triangulating on the third eye. Enter a state of stillness. In mental creation, nothing can be forced. If your mind is racing with thoughts, or if you feel agitated, remember that within each of us is a quiet pool of inner silence. Attune yourself to this and let any distractions go (they will go if you let them). Remember that we are not our thoughts. Thoughts pass through our mental landscape; only the ones we persistently hold to become a part of our existence. So, find the silence by letting the thought clutter slip away into the ether. . .

To quadralate, introduce a thought or an image into this empty space. Select something neutral: a flower garden, for instance. This starts as an abstract idea, but the mind will quickly begin to imagine a variety of flowers and colors and shapes.

With a certain relaxed detachment, watch as the mind proceeds in building up detail around the idea you have selected. A thought will automatically gather related thoughts and images until a very detailed structure accumulates around the original idea.

This is creation in action, and it is the same process by which a star is created in space. A seed thought acts as a point of gravitation, attracting related thoughts and gaining in mass, just as a gravitational point in space attracts dust and gas, eventually building up a huge amount of material around a center. Eventually the gravitational force of the accumulated mass generates so much heat and pressure that the mass ignites: a star is born and radiates its light into space. An idea follows the same stages of creation, eventually attracting so much mental energy/substance that it takes on form and becomes a visible, tangible event on the three-dimensional plane.

"A thought often makes us hotter than a fire."
Longfellow

"Nature is thought immersed in matter."
A. B. Alcott

161

"Points 1, 2, and 3 are fixed,
by your present definitions and standards,
but point 4 is flexible
and once we have located it,
then points 1, 2 and 3 become flexible too."

Points 1, 2 and 3 represent the three dimensions in which our bodies reside. Often the conditions of physical existence seem fixed, but freedom from these limitations lies in the ability of *MIND* to move into a higher dimension. This is an established mathematical principle - a limitation in one dimension can be overcome by moving into the next higher dimension where the limitation simply doesn't exist. The use of this law is the basis of innumerable books on positive thinking, self-help, etc.

> "The revelation of thought takes men out of servitude into freedom."
>
> Emerson

Try this exercise:

As always, stabilize your consciousness
by triangulating on the third eye.

Imagine yourself to be shrinking in size, like Alice, until you reach the size of an insect, perhaps an ant. Explore the area where you were sitting from the point of view of an ant. The chairs and desks that are sized to human proportions become monumental structures. Gravity is meaningless to a being that can walk "upside down" across a ceiling. Explore these new perceptions and compare the subjective differences between being ant-size and human-size.

Now try the other end of the size spectrum. Imagine yourself to be the size of a planet, wheeling in the vast reaches of space. Remember that a planet is aware. Explore the perceptions that a planet might have. Use no preconceived notions - simply place yourself in the position of a giant being in orbit around the sun and let yourself become aware of its perceptions - of space, of itself and its relation to the sun, of other stars and of who-knows-what - until you try.

Now return to your normal perception, but take the memory of your experiences in the fourth dimension with you. The essence of quadralating is to create, in imagery or thought-structure, a new subjective situation (ie. finding the flexible fourth point) which you then gradually transfer to normal awareness. Once accomplished, the seemingly fixed three-point awareness will automatically shift and flex to accommodate the the new fourth-point awareness. So, take the subjective changes in space that occurred when you viewed it from the perspective of an ant - or a planet - and make them a part of your mental equipment. We have actually created flexibility of height, width and depth by exploring alternate fourth points.

This next exercise takes us another step in quadralating by exploring the unseen, the unknown. Begin by selecting the empty space between any two objects (remember the teapot and cup, p.75). "Between each two material objects that you do perceive are minute variations on the curve where those combinations of coordinates do not appear as solid or perceptible to you, but exist nonetheless."

If you allow yourself to become receptive to these invisible areas by quadralating on them, you will begin to see something. Experiment on objects that are familiar in your everyday life.

This is an exercise you can do with eyes open or closed, but if you find that keeping your eyes open is distracting, try this: sit quietly and notice how the eyes will naturally focus on objects within the field of vision. Try to become aware of the energy current that flows through the eyes and out, into the world. As you begin to feel

> "A thought by thought is piled til some great truth is loosened..."
> Shelley

the current flowing, relax the eyes, let them unfocus, and begin to feel the current first slowing down, and then reversing. Once you have established this reversal (very easy to do) you will be in a state of triangulation with the eyes open. In other words, you will have temporarily disconnected the attachment to the three-dimensional world and can bring elements of the fourth dimension to the forefront of your awareness.

At first, as you practice gazing in between things, simply remain open to impresssions. These could take form as visual impressions or as fleeting thoughts. Persist and you will begin to catch glimpses of the invisible. Often, two or more people gazing in this way will "see" the same or similar things. This is very exciting, as it takes what you are doing out of the realm of vague imaginings and into the arena of a bold exploration, a venture into the unknown. When you are finished with the exercises, return to your normal consciousness.

> "The thoughts that come often unsought and, as it were, drop into the mind, are commonly the most valuable of any we have, and therefore should be secured, because they seldom return again."
> John Locke

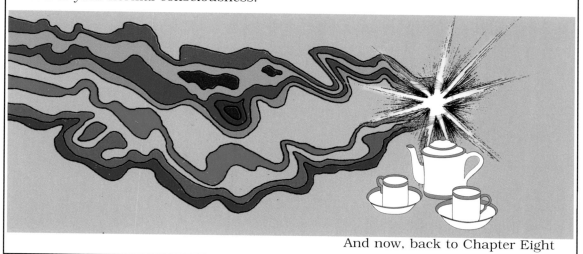

And now, back to Chapter Eight

163

ORIGINS

The origin of these sessions is the raw power of love that pulses through each of us. The largeness, the multifacets of these energy concept pools where we meet is greater than any one seemingly-isolated me. We are truly all interconnected. There is no end, no beginning to us individually. We are each a unique point in focus, constantly changing, never fixed, non-solid (though you appear solid), always interacting, being, as part

of a moving,

living,

changing

ALL.

"Is anything out there?"

You appear as singular units because that is the nature of an earth focus. For a moment the focus becomes *just itself*, a narrowed intense beam that appears isolated and individual, when in reality that focus, or that *you*, is an integral part of ALL THAT IS. It is ALL THAT IS. Without that focus, that you, there is no ALL THAT IS because every thing, *and every non-thing*, is ALL THAT IS ...

THE ALL cannot be minus ITSELF.

You cannot be *separate*, or, *only*,
or *not connected, uninvolved, alone.*

The experience
of being an individual
unit, singular and alone is
there to help your focus intensify and
create this specific you, this specific reality.
You must accurately feed your definition tapes with
knowledge Based on Truth, and Law.

When you KNOW the Oneness in ALL,
when you accept your totality,
then the invisible world becomes visible.

Small me self-involvement, or self-impor-
tance, implies separation. This is a misinterpreta-
tion of the truth that the ALL is within each one. The
small and too narrow focus then takes credit for ALL
THAT IS. The narrow focus tries to limit THE ALL by its
own meager definitions. This is done at the small-
me, ego level, the place where each one *narrows
down* and creates limits to feel safe, to feel secure
and familiar, as well as to specify and become.

At this point in time-space, the specfic earth
focus has become so narrowly defined that one can
actually *define oneself out of existence*, pull the cur-
tain and end the play by the sheer intensity of the
focus.

(We can see this intensity reflected in the various forms
of addictive behavior that warp and distort the natural
flow of the Life Energy that moves through the human
personality. These addictions - not just alcohol, or drugs,
but any obsessive belief system - can so constrict the
flow of the life force that it simply stops flowing through
that particular vehicle.)

Now is a good time to direct, plan, and shape your specific earth reality with wider, greater, more accurate definitions. An excellent way to begin redefining is with the simple act of tracing the origins and roots of words to see where the Law of THE ALL is visible. Almost any word root will give you a clue as to the BASIC meaning underneath the surface meaning. Consider the word "alone." The root is from the Middle English (ME) words "all" and "one." In common usage it means single, solitary or separate; in BASIC it shows that the individual originates from the ALL.

<u>ALONE</u>   [ME. all + one.]
Single; solitary; separate from others

<u>SEPARATE</u>   [L. se- APART + paro- PREPARE]
To prepare apart. To sever
(from inner connections),
divided from the rest
(of one's Self),
therefore   disjoined, not united, isolated.

The word "separate" means "isolated" or "divided from the rest," "not united." Its root is from the Latin words *"prepare apart."* The surface meaning describes a condition, but the root meaning implies a purpose. To separate is to pull apart from THE ALL, THE SOURCE, and create the specified, intense focus which allows you to become co-creators in shaping your own reality.

"O, sacred solitude! Divine retreat!
Choice of the prudent, envy of the great.
By thy pure stream, or in any waving shade,
We court fair wisdom, that celestial maid."
Edward Young

Hey,
where is everyone?
Am I ALONE?

As this process narrows the beam and intensifies the focus, you seem to <u>become</u> the focus, separate and alone.

In actuality you pare down in advance of the Return, the Union, the inevitable knowledge of your UNITY, YOUR ONENESS WITH ALL THAT IS.

In preparation for unity, each of you must meet your own misconceptions, such as self-involvement and self-reflection, to clear the channel and prepare the place for the new and accurate truth

Within.

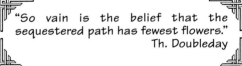

"So vain is the belief that the sequestered path has fewest flowers."
Th. Doubleday

Is the oak from the seed, or the seed from the oak? The seed and the oak are one, seemingly separate but in reality
ONE, ALL.

Neither comes first because 'comes first' is an isolated point only within the definition of Time. If Time is an illusion, then so is the concept of 'comes first.'

So we ask the question, where or what is *origin* if there is no 'comes first'?

> ORIGIN
> [L. **oriri**- TO ARISE, BE BORN,]
> *become visible.*
> [GR. **ormenos**- STIRRED UP]
> [Skt: **arnas**- (of waves) ROLLING]

Take away the definitions of time's limits and the Rolling Waves of Origin become:
ALL THAT IS,
ALL WAYS
ALWAYS

Once you have incorporated the new and broader definitions, the small and narrow focus of your earth view in THE EXPERIMENT will know Itself to be a part of ALL THAT IS and still retain its specified focus. The immensity of THE ALL is no threat to your specific earth focus. The raw power of ALL THAT IS cannot, will not destroy the small and narrow focus, for It creates the focus,
It IS the focus.

Life destroys only to create anew. The only destruction involved here is the breaking down of boundaries that are too limiting. Once free of the restrictions of narrow definitions, you may expand WITHIN, into worlds of wonder and delight: broad landscapes of design which are available and free for exploration by the bold and adventurous of spirit.

We are shaping the stage with new and expanded definitions of the idea of _limitless_. This is a safe idea, for although limits are necessary to create this focus (on the spoke), this reality, the present limitations set upon your use of awareness have become the prison bars of fear and superstition that impede you. Now is the time to go exploring, within, beyond this reality; beyond the specific focus limits of three-dimensional earth.

Your passport to freedom is our new definition of _limitless_, with which you may create and maintain a new and broader focus. You may consciously choose which limits to use as you learn to expand your awareness so that you may travel in the inner realms. Together we will explore the very concept of LIMITLESS.

You may define Origin as cause, as source,
but let the concept of _beginning_ go.

Let the _Tenets of Time-Space_
no longer fence you in.

Your control lies in the use of awareness, the conscious attention. With practice you will learn to keep a door open Within, to maintain an awareness level that is a state of *knowing.* Accumulated knowledge builds into structures of *knowing.* You build these structures into yourselves. You construct and can reconstruct the human form with your *knowing.*

The energy units which construct you are consciousness units also possessed of this function. One way you *know* is with word blocks, sound combinations which are the materials used to create, build and construct your bodies and your specific reality.

> **KNOW**
> [OE. cnawan- TO KNOW]
> to perceive directly; to have a clear and certain perception of a truth.

Knowing is the link between us, between all worlds. KNOW implies TRUTH. This link between Knowledge and Truth is a channel that flows from the open door Within to the alert outer consciousness anchored in Inner Knowledge and Truth. It is a link between inner and outer. It is a channel to the center of a

Spoke-Focus.

There are different channels through which major coordinates, archetypal structures flow. You, as individual focuses, choose certain channels through which to direct that flow.

One personality may express itself through the intellect, using words, sound blocks; another may use the channel of imagery, toned by definitions; others may use body language, or emotions.

All shape the flow.

Through any channel of a Spoke-Focus that you may choose for the expression of your individuality, there runs a center line, clear and straight, to the place of *knowing* within. This center line is your personal link to the never-ending well of inspiration, information, creativity and support that exists within each of you. It may seem at times as though the well lies hidden, and the flow of support, or creativity may seem to be sporadic or unpredictable.

However, it is within your power, by a simple shift of focus, to turn a sporadic flow into a steady, reliable spring that wells up from the Source of Knowing to guide and shape your every move.

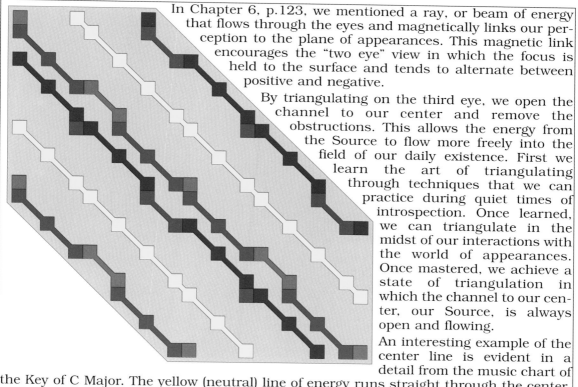

In Chapter 6, p.123, we mentioned a ray, or beam of energy that flows through the eyes and magnetically links our perception to the plane of appearances. This magnetic link encourages the "two eye" view in which the focus is held to the surface and tends to alternate between positive and negative.

By triangulating on the third eye, we open the channel to our center and remove the obstructions. This allows the energy from the Source to flow more freely into the field of our daily existence. First we learn the art of triangulating through techniques that we can practice during quiet times of introspection. Once learned, we can triangulate in the midst of our interactions with the world of appearances. Once mastered, we achieve a state of triangulation in which the channel to our center, our Source, is always open and flowing.

An interesting example of the center line is evident in a detail from the music chart of the Key of C Major. The yellow (neutral) line of energy runs straight through the center, and the alternating red (positive) and blue (negative) energies zig-zag on either side. As shown in the chart, the key to maintaining an open channel is neutrality. Event and circumstance (positive or negative) can strongly influence our subjective states of mind, but if we remember the *Reflector*, the mirror, we see that event and circumstance are a *reflection* of our subjective states, rather than the cause of them. This simple act shifts the focus from the outer appearance of opposites to an inner state of calm.

❖   ❖   ❖

In the alternating pulse of the red and blue, positive and negative energy flow of a music key you also see illustrated the pattern of duality that is an integral part of the earth focus.

This law of duality is one of the simple forms of Basic.

When the flow from the center of the Spoke-Focus moves through the *flat-plane* dimension of the earth reality, it appears to divide itself into dualities such as:

solid	nonsolid
matter	antimatter
visible	invisible
sensed	not sensed

However, because of the definition structure that limits your perception, non-solid *appears* to be non-existent. What reflects on the earth stage is a *one-sided image* so that polarities like solid - non-solid instead become visible in the solid aspects of:

positive	negative,
male	female,
selfconscious	subconscious
day	night

In actuality, there is no division.
There is only the appearance of two, the reality of One.
One of the challenges on earth, in this focus zone,
is to see past the appearance of the duality
and seek to unite the supposedly opposing forces.

The concept known as the *Mystic Marriage* represents the joining of the positive and negative elements within each person, in this case represented as your male and female sides.

When you join your own male and female qualities you can then extend this unity of self to encompass other aspects of the self -- your invisible side, your double, the other side of the mobius.

If you remember that everything seen with the two eyes is a *reflection*, then you will automatically assume the existence of the *Reflector*, the plane one coordinate place removed: the molding place, the place just prior to physical, material existence.

We are speaking here of the foundation of the Earth's corporealness, the astral plane, the formative world, the other side of the mobius.

You can begin to explore this by developing your conscious awareness of the interplay between visible and invisible. The music charts will aid in this.

Remember the color experiment in Chapter One, p.44, in which the color yellow represented the visible world and the gray area represented the invisible world? The color yellow, simply by its presence, caused the gray area to take on the opposite color, violet, thus increasing the intensity of the color yellow.

In the reflective medium of three-dimensional time-space earth, your every thought, word, mental image or deed is impressed into the gray area, the astral plane, enlarged or enhanced, and reflected into form. The shape, color and mood of your life is a reflection of your subjective states, both individually and collectively. As you see how visible and invisible are linked, you develop a degree of mastery over event and circumstance.

Just as the astral plane is the foundation of the visible world, in the music charts, the gray areas are the foundation of the visible colors.

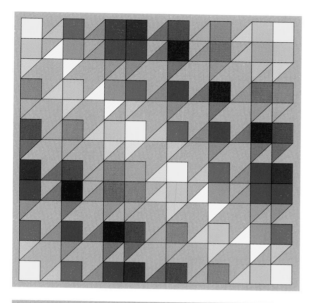

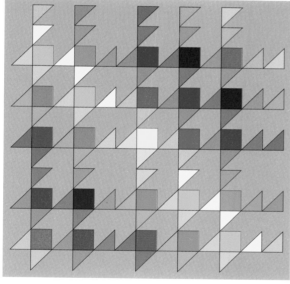

We painted the two charts on this page to experiment with the interplay between visible and invisible. On the page they are printed with both facing the same direction, but in our experiment, they are on opposite sides of a room, facing each other

The chart at the top is the E Major chart from Chapter One. The one below it is what we call the E Major negative chart. It is the reverse of the positive chart because the areas that are colored on the E Major positive chart are painted gray and the gray areas are painted in with their coresponding colors. When the two are placed across from each other they form a mobius energy flow.

The colors from the positive chart disappear into the gray areas of the negative chart, re-emerge as the colors in the negative chart which flow into the gray areas of the positive chart. . .a continuous energy loop between positive and negative, visible and invisible.

These charts illustrate the energy directed from both sides and flowing in both directions: between the 3rd and 4th dimensions, between solid and nonsolid, visible and invisible.

As you develop the awareness of the two sides of yourselves you need to remember that everything that is visible is also invisible.

Each is BOTH, and so, for our list:

SOLID	is	*NONSOLID*	is	SOLID
FEMALE	is	*MALE*	is	FEMALE
VISIBLE	is	*INVISIBLE*	is	VISIBLE
SENSED	is	*NOT SENSED*	is	SENSED

In the language of Basic the separation between solid and non-solid is an appearance only; yet, of course, the appearance is <u>based</u> on The LAW, and you may trace any appearance to its originating pulse, its mathematical coordinate.

We are speaking here of a simple few mathematical relations that are the Basic number structure of earth's reality. How simple are these number structures? In this age of computers, digital cameras and scanners, everything ever written, painted, photographed, or verbalized can be displayed on a computer screen. A computer uses what is called a binary language (code) to express all this and this code contains just two symbols, 0 and 1. Another example: collectively, we know hundreds of

thousands of words and we use them to describe concepts, plans, ideas, thoughts and feelings, and all this can be written with a mere handful of letters.

These number structures represent the substructure of words, images and sounds, which themselves are only descriptions of their *limits*, descriptions of their spectrum locations.

Words and sounds travel in one area of the spectrum. Mental images and thoughts travel in a *thinner, higher* area of this spectrum, on the other side of a line arbitrarily called the limit of visibility.

INVISIBLE TO TWO EYES, <u>VISIBLE</u> <u>TO</u> <u>THREE</u> <u>EYES</u>.

And so, as we come to the end of the PRIMER, we leave you with some reminders to aid you in your practice. Remember that the third eye is a functional organ in every human being. When you act on this premise, the eye begins to open, so. . .

PRACTICE SEEING THE UNSEEN.

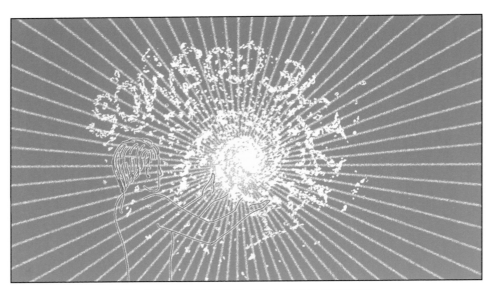

SEE ALL ON EARTH AS A REFLECTION.

Over and over we stress seeing the visible world as a reflection, for that act brings the invisible world to your attention and builds a rainbow bridge between the two.

When you cultivate the awareness that the other side is an integral part of this side, you will begin to see it, if you look.

START SEEING THE OTHER SIDE OF EVERYTHING IN ALL OF YOUR EVERYDAY ACTIONS AND INTERACTIONS.

TRAIN YOURSELF TO REMEMBER THAT YOU LIVE IN A REFLECTIVE REALITY.

With practice it will become evident.

REMEMBER
NEW

Triangulate to find a third point.
Quadralate to find a fourth.
Use the three eyes to see WITHIN to the invisible.

By triangulating on the third eye point, we open the gate into the invisible world.
By quadralating, we select our destination in that world
and energize our vehicle, our inner spaceship.

The exercises in perception that direct the mind to inner space form a parallel to the progression of dimensions that defines and constructs three-dimensional, or outer space. On the material plane, geometry has often served to explain that which cannot be directly perceived by reason or logic. According to the Pythagoreans, geometry, or Sacred Geometry as they knew it, is from the Archetypal Plane of Shape, the origin of the visible world. Sacred Geometry has been used by philosophers and seers to guide the student to perceive the meaning hidden within esoteric realms. With this in mind, notice that beginning with a point, each higher dimension can be generated by REFLECT-ING the preceding figure in a mirror. A point REFLECTED in a mirror gives the appearance of two points; this defines a line. A line REFLECTED at an angle forms two intersecting lines, a triangle. A right isoscles triangle REFLECTED in a mirror makes a perfect square. Tilt the mirror and a square begins to form a cube. In this way, through the process of reflection, the single point representing perfect UNITY is extended through the dimensions and into the field of physical manifestation.

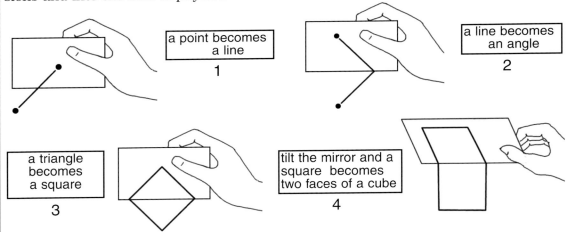

a point becomes
a line
1

a line becomes
an angle
2

a triangle
becomes
a square
3

tilt the mirror and a
square becomes
two faces of a cube
4

There's a common saying that goes, in effect, "That's not really magic - they did it all with mirrors." Common sense often reverses truth, and the truth is that real magic IS done with mirrors. Ancient Eastern philosophy, the bedrock on which many esoteric systems of thought are built, describes this as follows: the mind, it says, is like a lake, or pool of water. Thoughts passing through the mind ruffle its surface just as the pass-ing wind stirs up the surface of a lake. When the mind is stilled and the clutter of thought subsides, the mind becomes as smooth and reflective as a still pool, and the Light of Perfect Unity is reflected into the personal domain, the field of manifestation.

In essence, the reflective power of a mind stilled by triangulation performs a magical act. It consciously brings the light of creation across the Great Divide, from the unknowable...to the known.

In Quadralating we shape and focus the light to aid us in achieving our purpose.

Using an invisible tool
of the physical body,
the third eye,
to see into a thinner area
of the spectrum,

is travelling into the tube of a
Spoke-Focus to a faster rate of
vibration (the fourth dimension)
where _you_ _each_ _have_ the facility
to _see_, in-here.

We do this by quadralating.

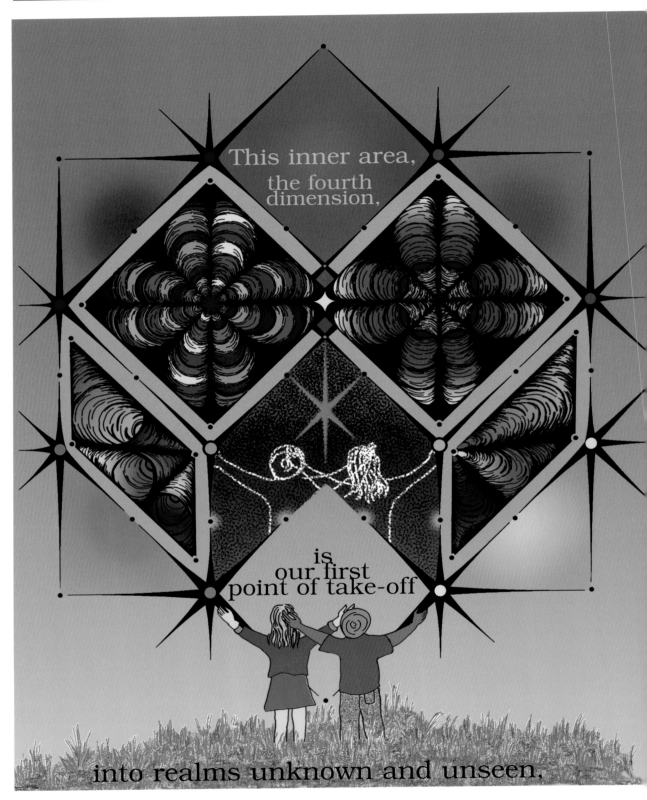

This inner area,
the fourth
dimension,

is
our first
point of take-off

into realms unknown and unseen,

THE TRAVELER'S REQUEST

Let me pass each lonely hour
Led by fate to the inner land
Where clocks and seasons tell me
After I've held the formless hand.

As all the lines that spell division
Are in actuality
Only phantom overlays
My inner sight will see.

AFTERWORD

For us, the authors and the publishers, THE PRIMER represents only the first six weeks of sessions in a book that was received over a three-year period. For you, our readers, we hope that THE PRIMER is the beginning of a journey that we will share for many years to come as we bring the notebooks of THE EXPERIMENT into published works.

It may seem as though THE PRIMER plunges you head first into the water, and in a sense, it does. It introduces the reader in broad sweeps to the material that lies ahead - inner space travel, the fourth dimension, triangulating and quadralating, *reflection* and *Reflector*, the Spoke-Focus shape of reality. It all may seem a little strange and new, but if you stick with us, we can promise you a fascinating and illuminating journey.

If you are feeling a little overwhelmed at the prospect of developing the third eye into a functioning tool of perception and travelling the inner realms, rest assured that we felt the same way when this material first came through. But after weeks and months of sessions, we began to relax as we saw that our teachers were slowly and surely educating us to a new point of view in our circling strolls around the *concept pool*.

In the coming books we will continue our strolls, and as we circle the pool, we spiral in to an understanding of who we are, how we perceive this reality we call three-dimensional earth, and how our power to focus, shapes the reflective medium of time-space into the experience we call life.

For now we begin to develop our vehicle, our inner spaceship, by triangulating on the third eye and quadralating on various fourth points. Use the exercises in the book as a starting point and develop your own variations. Try visiting a familiar location in quadralating to see what is there when viewed from the other side of the mobius. Do this with a friend and you may be amazed to find that you both are seeing the same, or similar, sights.

The music charts and the seven star charts (see Appendix A, facing page) are a key part of THE EXPERIMENT. These charts are magical. Just being within the field of their energy begins a process that goes on beneath the surface of our consciousness and works invisibly to bring us into alignment with the harmonious forces of the cosmos. They are the catalyst that spark imagination and information into growth and progress. They are available from our website, **www.theakademe.com**.

Finally, we wish you well in your discovery and
exploration of the inner realms that await you.

APPENDIX A   THE COLOR CHARTS

The color charts of the keys of music and of the SevenStar designs are the heart of THE EXPERIMENT. When the teachers urged us to begin work on these paintings, they told us that the charts would change our lives in ways we couldn't even imagine. We soon found what they said to be true, and after twenty years of living with them and exploring their variations, we are still discovering new depths to our experience of the charts.

If you have been touched by what you have read and seen in these pages, we urge you to add some charts to your environment. Imagine living in an environment that is shaped and directed to enhance the harmony of color and

music. As the charts go up in your house, they beam that energy into your life and you begin to resonate with the harmonies they project. That subtle alignment within you shapes the life force that flows through you into patterns of harmony which will reflect in the events and circumstances of your life experience.

CHART OF THE KEY OF E MAJOR
This chart is based on the sound of the note of E natural (yellow) and the surrounding notes and colors of the key of E Major.
Yellow is a neutral color, neither warm nor cool. It is a non-moving color, therefore it is good for centering, and achieving a state of neutrality and balance.

CHART OF THE KEY OF C MAJOR
The chart of the key of C Major is a very powerful chart. Red is the first spectral color, warm and very stimulating.
It represents motion away from the viewer, outward, into the world. Red is the color of the Mars force. When it is in harmony, as in the chart, all outward expressions of power are balanced.

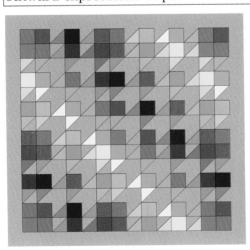

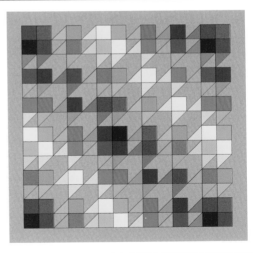

CHART OF THE KEY OF G# MAJOR
G# Major is the musical key that expresses the harmonies of the color blue. This color is cool and calming. It represents motion inward, toward the viewer. In that capacity, this chart aids in meditation, introspection and inner balance.

MAJOR SCALE NEGATIVE CHARTS

This page displays the charts that we think of as the invisible side of the Major scale charts shown on the previous page. Taken together, each pair of charts, positive and negative, completes a cycle of energy that flows from visible to invisible and back again. For an example in the text, see p. *175.*

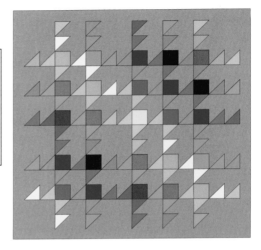

CHART OF THE KEY OF E MAJOR (NEGATIVE)

This chart is the opposite, or mobius companion to the E Major Chart. Rather than thinking of this pair as opposites in terms of conflicting sides, the positive and negative charts are complementary; taken together, they present the separate parts that make the whole.

CHART OF THE KEY OF C MAJOR (NEGATIVE)

This chart is the pair to the Key of C Major (Positive) on the preceding page. As you can see, these negative charts are like a skeleton upon which the fully fleshed out (positive) charts are built.

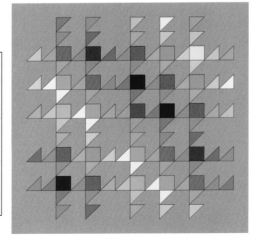

CHART OF THE KEY OF G# MAJOR (NEGATIVE)

Just as a skeleton is the invisible support system of the body, the negative side of each chart supports the positive aspect. When the two charts are placed facing each other, they stimulate the flow of energy between the visible and invisible aspects of the color or musical key that is illustrated. This, in turn, stimulates the flow of energy between the visible and invisible aspects of ourselves and helps to balance the positive and negative poles within and around us.

E MAJOR STAR

A combination of four E Major charts, each one raying out in a different direction to make a starburst pattern. The "Trademark" Spoke-Focus chart. (See p. 62) Just as a star radiates light and warmth, this chart sends its energy throughout the area in which it is placed. (Available in different sizes)

E MAJOR POSITIVE AND NEGATIVE

This chart is a union of the two aspects of the E Major Chart. Just looking at it every day will help to balance the positive and negative, male and female, solid and non-solid aspects of the personality. Some of those who have advance copies of this chart have remarked that they experienced a greater control over their emotions when they started looking at the chart every day.

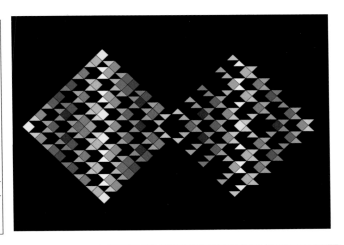

10 TRIANGLE CHART

A grid of equilateral triangles has been used for thousands of years to represent the mathematical principles of order and harmony underlying the formation of the Cosmos.

In THE EXPERIMENT, the ten triangle chart is based on that grid and is used as a tool for helping perception to shift between the four facets of focus. A set of simple exercises accompanies the chart and aids in moving consciousness between layers of awareness. (see Glossary, Four Facets of Focus, p. *202*, see also p. *110* and p. *147*)

The exercises are deceptively simple since consciously moving your perception between layers sends a powerful signal to yourself that these other layers are available to you, and that initiates a process that begins to funnel information from these other layers to your conscious level of awareness.

THE THREE OF US

The triple oval chart in the SevenStar series called "The Three of Us" is a powerful chart with multilayered effects. At one level, it simply radiates an energy wind that sweeps clean the area in which it is placed. Guests who have slept under it (it's in the living room, over the couch and measures 5' x 10') have never failed

to wake up without having experienced vivid dreams, transformational encounters or some type of heightened awareness. It has powerful properties - physical and mental. It has stimulated psychic activity in some viewers. We welcome your feedback on our website, **www.theakademe.com**.

SEVENSTAR OVAL

A complex chart that is the root of many different charts and grids. The oval is a two-dimensional representation of the shape associated with the human energy body. The introduction of the number seven into a field of twelve (colors) gives rise to a delicate imbalance (the 7:5 proportion) that is the source of creativity, art and spiritual unfoldment. By contrast, the division of twelve into six and six represents perfect balance and order, but also a certain lack of motion. The correspondences in the SevenStar charts point up many relationships between color and number and between complementary opposite colors.

SEVENSTAR GRID

Another variation of the SevenStar pattern, a grid of stars in a repeating pattern. Very effective in energizing and aligning the viewer, especially when two or four charts are arranged together to produce a larger pattern.

THE AKADEME

The Akademe was established to spread the teachings from the concept pool as heard and recorded by Ketherin Michaels during her sessions with the Inner Teachers. The Akademe's primary purpose is to publish the notebooks of The Experiment, but there is also a wealth of imagery that is available through the website, at **www.theakademe.com**.

Learning has always been transmitted orally, from person to person, but with the invention of printing, information became more widely available. Now, as we enter another stage of development, images are becoming a more important medium used to transmit information. An image bypasses the logical, analytical side of the brain, the side that assembles the meaning found in words, and is grasped immediately, without explanation. The Teachers often speak of this capacity of the brain to directly assimilate images as part of the mental equipment we are refining in the New Age.

The charts have the power to effect changes in us by going directly to the visual centers in the brain.

> "Use the charts to store colors. Feed the eye with balanced light. The eye takes in the color and the brain stores it, and, as an actual nourishment, the vibration reverberates through and is assimilated into the body. Looking at the charts fills up the body with color until it overflows. It is an inundation of aligned color, an internal bath of flowing, ordered vibrations." (from p. *101*)

The charts shown on the preceding pages are available on the Akademe's website. Other patterns, designs and images from the book will become available as posters or T-shirts. The major keys of the three primary colors, red, C-major, blue, G-major and yellow, E-major are shown here in Positive and Negative but each of the keys has its chart, in Major and Minor scale variations. As each key of music has a mood tone, so does each chart. The SevenStar charts likewise travel into many variations and color patterns.

You may reach The Akademe at our website, at **www.theakademe.com**. It is primarily, an online academy of higher learning. New information will be posted there as it becomes available. You may also contact The Akademe in care of:

GreyBear Publishing Co
PO Box 5158
Santa Fe, NM 87502

APPENDIX B   LIGHT AND COLOR

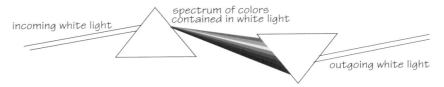

The solar spectrum (above) shows the colors that emerge from sunlight when it is refracted through raindrops to create the vision of a rainbow, or through a prism as in Isaac Newton's famous experiment.

incoming white light

spectrum of colors
contained in white light

outgoing white light

These colors can be separated from sunlight, as in the first prism, and they can also be recombined into clear light by passing them through a second prism.

When it comes to vision, there is an important distinction between the two types of color perception, one being the direct perception of light emitted from a radiant source (the sun, stars, or artificial light sources), and the other being the perception of light that has been reflected from the surface of an object. Television uses the former system; called *additive* because it adds colored light in various proportions to make up the colors we see on screen. The system that describes how the eye sees the objects around us is called *subtractive.* It works like this: white light, which contains within itself all the hues of color, shines on an object within our view. Some of the color in the light is *absorbed* by the pigments on the surface of the object or *subtracted* from view; the rest is reflected to the eye. The reflected part is the color we see.

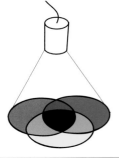

<u>Additive system</u>	<u>Subtractive system</u>
of color perception. As more colored lights are added, the colors get lighter. In the center, where all the colors are mixed together, the perception is of all color, or white, similar to Newton's experiment in which all the colors from the first prism were merged in the second prism to create clear, or white light.	of color perception. This is the system that represents how we see physical objects. It depends upon the quality of pigments to selectively absorb and reflect light. When subjected to white light containing all colors, a pigment will absorb some of the colors and reflect some. The color we see is the wavelength that is reflected. As more pigments are mixed, more color is absorbed and the color in the center gets darker. Since more light is subtracted with each pigment, the end result is the absence of color, black.

What is subtracted or absorbed is invisible to the eye. Our discussion of color throughout this book has focused almost exclusively on how the eye perceives *reflected* light as that is how the physical world becomes visible to us: through reflection.

The classical view of the solar spectrum since the time of Newton (or before) is of a seven color spectrum, but the essence of this spectrum is just three colors, red, yellow and blue, the primary colors. While there may be some controversy over what constitutes a primary color, it is clear that in pigments, these colors cannot be reduced to anything more basic. True yellow, blue and red cannot be expressed as a mixture of other colors, and, given pigments of ideal purity and transparency, any color imaginable can be produced from them. For this reason, artists have always called these the primary colors and they are at the heart of the artist's color wheel.

The wheel just outside the primaries contains six colors, three of them the primary colors, and three secondary colors: green, orange and violet. These colors are called secondary because each is a mixture of two primary colors (1 + 1 = 2). Green, for instance is a blend of yellow and blue. On the wheel, green is positioned between those two primary colors, and so it is with the other secondary colors. Orange is between red and yellow, and violet is between blue and red. Each secondary color is a mixture of the two primary colors next to it on the wheel.

The full color wheel has a third circle which contains, not surprisingly, tertiary colors. These are mixtures of a primary color and a secondary color (1 + 2 = 3), and are named accordingly: red, a primary, plus orange, a secondary, mix to create red-orange, a tertiary. Between each primary and secondary on the outer wheel is a tertiary, a mixture of the two colors to either side of it. Hence red-violet is a mixture of red and violet, blue-green is a mixture of blue and green and so on.

The diagram on the following page shows a full-page artist's color wheel with the bar at the top showing the creation of the secondaries from the three primaries. The bar at the bottom shows the formation of the tertiary colors from the mixture of the primaries and secondaries.

The structure of the diagram shows arms branching out from each color and mixing to create the next level of color from the primaries to the secondaries to the tertiaries. This colorwheel will be available as a poster for it shows the incredible order and harmony that is at the heart of our power of vision. (See p. 191 for more information about The Akademe and the website **www.theakademe.com**)

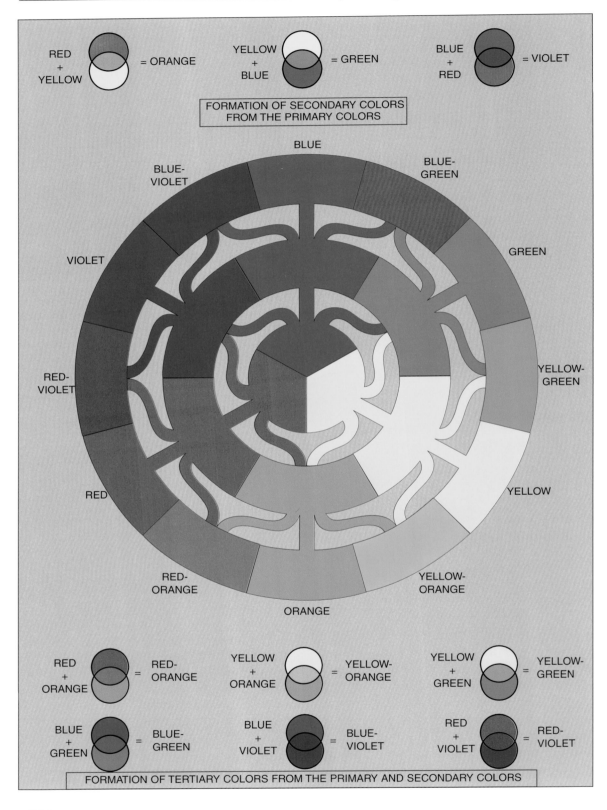

RED + YELLOW = ORANGE

YELLOW + BLUE = GREEN

BLUE + RED = VIOLET

FORMATION OF SECONDARY COLORS
FROM THE PRIMARY COLORS

BLUE

BLUE-VIOLET

BLUE-GREEN

VIOLET

GREEN

RED-VIOLET

YELLOW-GREEN

RED

YELLOW

RED-ORANGE

YELLOW-ORANGE

ORANGE

RED + ORANGE = RED-ORANGE

YELLOW + ORANGE = YELLOW-ORANGE

YELLOW + GREEN = YELLOW-GREEN

BLUE + GREEN = BLUE-GREEN

BLUE + VIOLET = BLUE-VIOLET

RED + VIOLET = RED-VIOLET

FORMATION OF TERTIARY COLORS FROM THE PRIMARY AND SECONDARY COLORS

APPENDIX C   THE SPOKE-FOCUS

The Spoke-Focus shape represents the connections that link one with all. It has been noted that the ALL is in the one - that each single speck contains the knowledge of the whole, and the network described by the Spoke-Focus is the cosmic internet that links all the parts and makes them WHOLE.

The individual links are endless - our whole existence is given meaning through the connections that join us. The body is a network of cells, of blood vessels, of nerves that is constantly communicating and sharing information. As individuals, our lives acquire meaning through our connections - with family members, business associates, with the network of goods and services that provides us food and shelter, with the books and information that keep the knowledge, wit and wisdom of the past active in the present.

The entire story of our development, from children to adults, from simple, isolated societies to a globally interlinked culture, from earthbound to star travellers is the story of exploring and developing the links that provide the means to move into wider and deeper fields of endeavor.

As we read THE EXPERIMENT we begin to develop the hidden connections that link us with Spirit, Cosmic Consciousness, the *Reflector*. We can enhance this with a series of visualizations that recognize the connections that support us and move on to the connections through which we support others, not just other people but the earth, the animals, the plants. Every breath we take supports our cellular structure and every breath we release supports the plant kingdom and through it the animal kingdom, in and out throughout the earth. The body of the earth and all things on it, in it, are linked in an energy exchange, and if our very breath reaches out to touch all things that live, how much more so our conscious thoughts, actions and words?

Our slightest thought, word or deed ripples in everwidening circles throughout the network that joins us. When a thought or an image is focused, or held in a meditation, it acquires force and momentum. This is our greatest power and our great legacy, for as we develop the power to focus and direct energy, we can affect events and people that appear to be unconnected.

As this book is going to press, the twin towers of New York have fallen and the earth is poised on the brink. Of what is still uncertain. What is certain is that we have the power, as individuals, to affect the balance of events and circumstances.

In a meditation, or a silent moment, feel your connection with the earth. See yourself as part of the Spoke-Focus of life. Begin with a point of consciousness, you, and feel the flow that joins you with the plants, the animals, the rocks, your fellow humans, all the beings of the earth, the solar system and beyond, to the limitless ALL. Remember that you are a center of expression for the Cosmic Will to Good. Then let that energy flow through you, shaped by your feeling of love for the earth, for the beauty of life and for the wonder of existence. Feel the energy flow outward to infuse the network of life with a glow of light.

The ideas suggested by the term "Spoke-Focus" can be further explored by the definitions and images associated with the words "spoke" and "focus."

SPOKE

[ME. Spake - Radius or ray of a wheel;
past tense of speak.]

The radius or ray of a wheel.
Any of the small bars
inserted in the hub
which serve to support the rim.

SPEAK
[from the Sanskrit: Sphurjati:
roars, CRACKLES]
to utter words, to articulate
sound, to pronounce or express
orally.

"Thirty spokes share the wheel's hub; it is
the center that makes it useful."
Lao Tsu

SPEECH defines.

WORDS enclose fields of
consciousness.

Mahatma Ghandi worked daily
at the spinning wheel, which
came to symbolize India's aspirations for independence.

SOUND
The sensation of hearing due
to the stimulation
of the auditory nerves
and centers of the brain,
usually by VIBRATIONS transmitted through the air.

The Moirai,
Greek Goddesses of fate,
who spun thread
on the wheel of human life:
Clotho, the spinner,
Lachesis, the disposer of lots,
Atropos, who cuts the thread.

"And endless are the modes of
speech, and far Extends from side
to side the field of words."
Homer

"Speak not at all, in any wise,
till you have somewhat to speak;
care not for the reward
of your speaking,
but simply and with undivided mind
for the truth of your speaking."
Carlyle

"In the Beginning was the Word."

"Speech is but broken light
upon the depth
of the unspoken"
George Eliot

"Speech being even three times greater
than the sense of hearing or of sight;
that is the highest vibration we have in
the body at all."
Edgar Cayce

FOCUS

[L. Focus:- Fireplace; hearth.]

A central or gathering point,
as a fireplace or hearth.

A center of concentration or
point of greatest energy.

In optics,
a point at which rays
of light converge
or from which they diverge.

The adjustment necessary
to produce a clear image.

Vasati

[Sanskrit: he dwells.]

In acoustics, the point toward which the
sound waves converge.

KEEP THE HOME
FIRES BURNING.

"Everything that gives light
is dependent upon something
to which it clings
in order that it may
continue to shine."
Li, The Clinging, Fire
I Ching

Kepler's mathematical focus
of a curve is as
the burning point of a lens.

"The fire in the flint shows not till it be
struck."
- Timon of Athens
Shakespeare

HESTIA

Greek Virgin Goddess of the Hearth.
One of the twelve Great Olympians
Keeper of the Sacred Flame
Guardian of Home and Hearth.

VESTA
Roman Virgin Goddess
of hearth and fire.

Vestal Virgins were consecrated
to Vesta and the service
of watching the sacred fire
which was perpetually kept burning
upon Her altar.

"Hestia, in all dwellings
of men and immortals
Yours is the highest honor,
the sweet wine offered.
First and last at the feast,
poured out to You duly.
Never without You
can gods or mortals hold banquet."

The SPOKE-FOCUS image shows a series of focus points with spokes radiating out (or in) from each centerpoint.

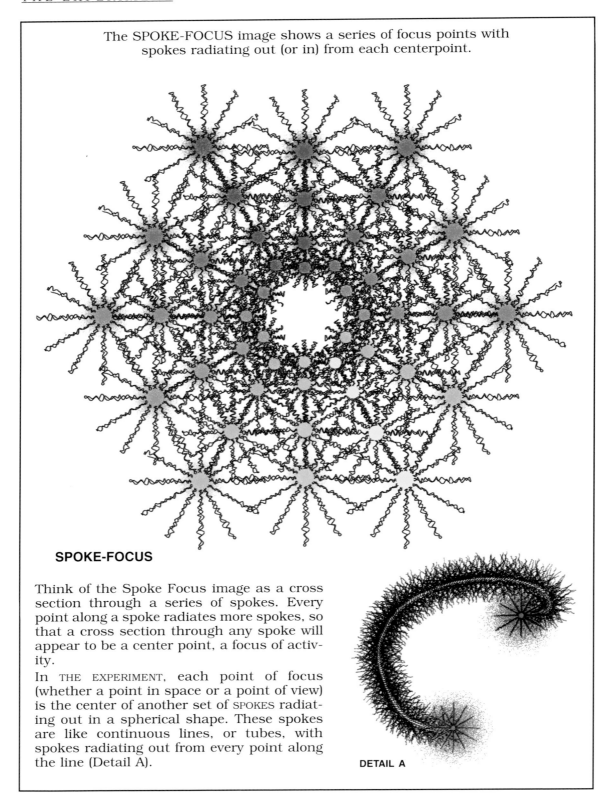

SPOKE-FOCUS

Think of the Spoke Focus image as a cross section through a series of spokes. Every point along a spoke radiates more spokes, so that a cross section through any spoke will appear to be a center point, a focus of activity.

In THE EXPERIMENT, each point of focus (whether a point in space or a point of view) is the center of another set of SPOKES radiating out in a spherical shape. These spokes are like continuous lines, or tubes, with spokes radiating out from every point along the line (Detail A).

DETAIL A

This idea of Spokes seems reminiscent of the early "string" theories in physics which speculated that subatomic particles may be aspects of vibrating strings which have their full existence in ten dimensions. Since we are perceiving from the standpoint of the third dimension, we see only the aspect of the "string" that appears in our flat-plane view and so call it a particle, a point.

Consider the following passage from *The Fire From Within*, by Carlos Castaneda, in relation to the Spokes of Creation. His teacher, Don Juan, is describing to Castaneda his impression of the emanations at large, the emanations of existence.

" 'Are the emanations like beams of light?' I asked.

" 'No. Not at all. That would be too simple. They are something indescribable. And yet, my personal comment would be to say that they are like filaments of light. What's incomprehensible to normal awareness is that the filaments are aware. I can't tell you what that means, because I don't know what I'm saying. All I can tell you with my personal comments is that the filaments are aware of themselves, alive and vibrating, that there are so many of them that numbers have no meaning and that each of them is an eternity in itself.' "

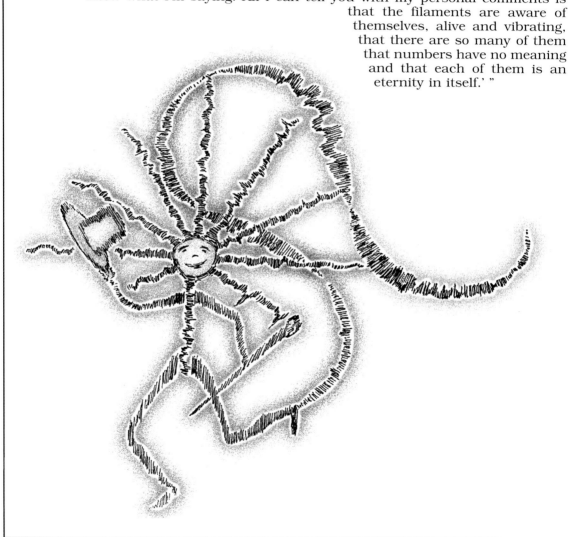

GLOSSARY

Angle variance   In THE EXPERIMENT, Chapter 6, angle variance is defined as "the degree on the curve of space at which a point manifests." The angle variance of a point is what determines how that point appears to one's perception. This may seem an abstruse concept, but think of angle variance in terms of a simple, holographic image that changes appearance as you change the angle at which it is viewed. This is a simple form of angle variation. Another familiar aspect of angle variance is seen in the way one may resolve a situation by approaching it from a different angle - change the angle, and the whole situation shifts. In THE EXPERIMENT the sensory experience of three-dimensional earth reality occurs within a range of angle variation that is analogous to the way that vision occurs within a certain range of light frequencies. In the absence of visible light, we see nothing. Anything that falls outside the range of angle variation we are programmed to perceive simply doesn't exist for us. Since aspects of overlapping realities are all around us, interpenetrating the same time and space (remember the view through the crystal, p. 56-57), the way our perception limits the earth experience to just one of these aspects is called an **angle distortion**.

Attention   Attention and intention, or intent, are two sides of a single concept. The root of both words is the Latin word *tendo* meaning "to stretch." Attention is a stretching outward and intention is a stretching inward. Both actions are directed by **focus**. We focus our attention on something outside of ourselves, but what, exactly are we focusing? Many esoteric traditions describe the body, the personality, the human being, as an aggregate, a coming together of parts that is held together by the life force that flows through it. This vital substance, the life force, is what we focus when we bring our attention to bear on anything.

Basic   A language of ideas or concepts that penetrates through layers of reality to bring hidden meanings to the surface of consciousness. One example of using Basic is to look in a dictionary at the root definitions of words to bring up layers of meaning that may have become obscured or overlooked. We shape sound by the words we choose and speech is a powerful tool we use in shaping reality. Knowing the underlying meanings of the words we use extends that power. The word "consider" illustrates this. We *consider* the angles before coming to a decision. The root of "consider" is the Latin *con*, with, and *sider*, star. In our reality, a star is the source of warmth, of light, of energy, of life itself. What we actually do when we consider the aspects of a situation before coming to a decision is to align ourselves with the source of life and power. In a carefully considered decision, the life-power flows through us, taking shape in the effects of our choice. This is Basic at work in our lives, multidimensional, multilayered. The teachers urge us to see the world around us as it is described in Basic to get to the essence of our experience by applying The Law, the idea that all things come from the ONE.

Concept pool   A pool of ideas. In THE EXPERIMENT, our strolls around the concept pool expose us to ideas that stretch our perception. This has similarities to the Platonic conception of an archetypal plane of pure thought or idea that holds the ideal patterns which unfold into all aspects of earthly experience.

Curve of Space   In Einstein's conception of physics, all space is curved and all motion is spiral. In THE EXPERIMENT, each **spoke focus** is a continuous curve containing all the mathematically possible variations within it. Aspects or layers of reality, or perception, are found along the curve at varying angles or degrees, and the definition limits associated with a specific set of curve coordinates determine how that reality or aspect of perception will appear (Chapter Two, The Shape of Reality, p. 65-66) (see also **angle variance**). In Chapter Five, the curve of space is said to be a **mobius strip**. Like the mobius, the curve of space has two sides, but one continuous surface. Although the surface is continuous, single, perception as we know it tends to be focused on one side of the strip, or surface. This gives rise to the idea of "the other," "the other side," "the double." As we learn to expand our perception beyond the limits of "this side only," we become aware of both sides of the curve; we clear the channel to the center of the Spoke-Focus and incorporate the two sides of the curve into one, continuous surface. Once we accomplish this, at whatever level, information from the system of probables that surrounds us becomes available consciously.

Flat plane The myth (of the flat plane) has persisted through common usage since before the time that the earth was thought to be flat. The illusion persists in our minds because of the way things appear to the perception. For instance, in our buildings, we attempt to achieve flat planes for our floors, walls, etc even though we know that space is curved. Within our limited viewpoint, however, flatness seems achievable and desirable. Another example: when we wish to convey an idea or an image, we mark it down on paper, another flat plane. We would be hard pressed to sculpt an image of what we wanted to express instead of sketching it out with pencil and paper. Consider a set of architectural plans. For a complex building the plans could run to hundreds of pages, but within those pages, every detail of the building could be represented. A model could conceivably be made to represent all aspects of the building, but even then, our minds would want to break each stage down to its flat-plane, straight-line components in order to assimilate its meaning. We see, think and operate in flat-plane terms. What the teachers in THE EXPERIMENT would have us do is stretch the boundaries of our perception beyond the illusion of the flat-plane appearance to become aware that though the appearance of things may be flat-planed, the reality is spherical. See Chapter Two, the Shape of Reality (p. 60-63), Chapter Six, Triangulation (p. 122-123), and Chapter Seven, Crystals and Minerals (p 144-146), for more on this.

Scientists have been forced into this type of thinking by their discoveries about the nature of subatomic particles. At first, the standard view of the atom was of a central nucleus with a certain number of electrons orbiting the central mass, much like our conception of the Solar System with the planets orbiting the sun, each one traveling an elliptical path that is essentially contained within a flat plane. However, as quantum mechanics replaced the classical view, scientists realized that the electron they thought was a discrete, specific particle in one place at a time was more accurately described as a cloud of probable electron energy dispersed throughout a spherical shell. The electron only "appeared" as a particle when scientists focused their perception on it. When they brought the "electron" within the boundaries of their perception, they collapsed the spherical quality and it then appeared as solid. The Experiment asks us to perform a similar feat of mental gymnastics by recognizing that the world we consider as solid and real is only so because we are habituated to perceiving it so. It asks us to remember the probable nature of existence rather than insisting on the singular view. This is greatly to our benefit. In the linear, flat-plane view, one event follows inexorably after the previous event, everything determined by what came before. In the spherical view, each event has a probability of occurring, along with every other possible permutation of the event. We then pluck events from the field of probables in a spontaneous dance of being, rather than trudging through a predetermined line of events and circumstances.

This may seem abstract, and it is, but it is also very practical and useful. By loosening our grip on the hard and fast flat-plane interpretation of reality, we allow a sense of freedom into our existence. No longer does the past grimly determine the present and future. In a system of probables, we place our focus upon the ideal (the ideal life, the ideal outcome) and that ideal (future) magnetically attracts us to it. In other words, the future, which we consider to be open and unconstrained, full of possibility and hope, is what creates the present. Consider the spherical, probable nature of reality and look for the evidence. It will appear.

Focus   In eyesight, the ability of the lens to bend the incoming rays of light so they meet at a point (on the retina). The power to bring the awareness to bear upon a set of variables and so create and experience a reality. Just as a lens concentrates rays of sunlight in a burning point of fire, focusing our attention on a thought or an idea concentrates a very real force, which, over time, transforms the invisible thought into solid, three-dimensional form.

The power of focus is the finest tool at our disposal. With it, we sculpt the form and the details of our personal existence. Imagine a fairy godmother wandering through a great hall with tables and counters stacked with sheets of paper - each one covered with images. She browses through the hall, touching now one and now another of the images with her wand and as her power flows into the image, it takes on three-dimensional form and rises up, animated, active, alive. Focus works just like that. It is our magic wand. The images are the thoughts that flow through the mind. As we focus our conscious **attention** on a thought, the thought becomes more powerful, and it begins to take on form, ephemeral at first, but over time, the thought will be drawn into form in three dimensions.

Four facets of focus   This concept is dealt with in the next volume of THE EXPERIMENT, but it has been introduced in association with the ten triangle diagram shown in Chapter Seven and in Appendix A, The Color Charts. The four facets are ways of tuning the perception to focus on different aspects. For instance the ten triangles can be seen as flat-plane triangles or three-dimensionally, as two cubes. A third form would be two interlocking hexagons and a fourth would be a pair of spinning wheels. Mental shifts occur when consciously changing between the four views. Instructions come with chart.

Fourth dimension   In science and particularly in the theory of relativity, time is the fourth dimension. In THE EXPERIMENT, time is considered to be a feature of our experience in three dimensions. The fourth dimension, as used in THE EXPERIMENT, refers to the world of thought, a world free from the limitations of time and space, a world of probables.

Imagin   To use the power of focus in mental creation. To consciously shape the universal life energy with our imagery to achieve our desires, to realize our goals, to form our reality.

Intent   The force of Will. At the Cosmic level, intent is the purpose of ALL THAT IS. On a personal level intent is our purpose, our determination. It is said that the ideal state to achieve at the self-conscious level is transparency. In this condition, the intent, or will, of ALL THAT IS flows through us undistorted and takes form in a reality that perfectly expresses our fullest potential. In this state, the personal is merged with the divine, and this represents the perfected life, achieved by personalities like Buddha or Jesus. At the personal level, intent is the force that accomplishes everything that we do. Once we "make up our mind" to do something, it often just happens, seemingly without effort. This is the force of intent at work.

Inner space   An inner mental landscape as rich and varied as anything in three-dimensional space. Open to exploration using the mind, the third eye and the inner spaceship.

Inner spaceship   A vehicle we create using breath, color, the third eye and the power of **imagin**. A vehicle we can use to safely travel the inner realms.

Law of Polarity   The Law of Polarity states that opposites are identical in nature, but different in degree. For instance, heat and cold are extremes of temperature, far and near are extremes of distance, ecstacy and despair are extremes of emotion. Any condition that exists can be located somewhere on a scale between a pair of opposing values. That is the nature of living in a world dominated by dualities. The advantage of this system is that conditions can be easily influenced to move along the scale toward one pole or the other. One only needs to focus on the desired quality in order to achieve movement in that direction. The authors of *The Kybalion* (see Bibliography) note that to change something's essential nature, for instance, from what is distant to what is orange, would be a feat indeed, but that to change something's position along a line of movement from one pole to the other is much simpler (for instance, to move toward what is far brings it near).

Mirror blind   The condition of acting as though the world of appearances, of sensory perception, is the only reality. In contrast to that, **mirror living** refers to the knowledge that the world of sensory perception is a stage setting and that as Players, we have an existence off stage as well. Mirror living develops the view that we can become conscious of both sides of the mirror, the *reflection* <u>and</u> the *Reflector*.

Mobius strip   A geometrical or topological figure named after the German scientist (August Mobius) who is said to have discovered it. It is formed by taking a rectangular strip (of paper) and putting in a half twist before joining the ends together. This twist has the effect of turning a strip with two surfaces and two edges into a figure with just one surface and one edge. Because of its startling properties, the mobius strip has become a symbol for the way that a simple transformation can reveal a magical, baffling (to the mirror blind) aspect of nature. (See Chapter Five, The Shape of the Flow, for more on the mobius strip. Also, see the end of Chapter Seven, Crystals and Minerals, for a mental exercise involving the mobius strip, p. 149.)

Perception   A mysterious process by which we assemble the energy that surrounds us into a coherent, more or less consistent structure. No one explains this better than don Juan, in Castaneda's seventh book, *The Fire From Within*, an inspiring, exciting account of the nature of awareness (see bibliograpy).

Platonic solids   A group of five geometric solids (tetrahedron, cube, octahedron, icosahedron and dodecahedron) discovered by Pythagoras and his followers that represent the ideal of shape in three dimensions of space. These shapes are templates for the geometric structure of crystal and mineral formation (see Chapter Seven, Crystals and Minerals; see also Bibliography *Minerals of the World: A Guide to Field Identification*).

Pythagoras   A Greek philosopher, scientist, mathematician, seer of the 5th Century B.C. whose explorations of nature, vibration and consciousness laid the foundations for modern studies in sound vibration, geometry, mathematics and the occult significance of number and shape.

Quadralating   Triangulating and quadralating are a pair of terms that describe how we can use the power of focus to become aware of, and travel through, layers or aspects of reality. By triangulating, we construct our take-off dock, the launch pad to inner space. By quadralating, we select a destination and energize the inner spaceship for travel into the fourth dimension. To quadralate is to mentally "lock on" to a probable destination and bring it into the field of perception.

Reality   A term loosely used to refer to that which lies within the range of our senses, inner and outer. One's reality is that which is contained within the bubble of perception, to use a don Juan term. Outside the bubble is the *unknown*, and beyond that, the *unknowable*. As we develop the acuity of our senses, both outer and inner, we expand the range of our perception by bringing aspects of the unknown into the realm of the known. However it is the nature of human existence on earth to operate within certain limitations; to say that reality is ALL THAT IS may be true but it's also a concept that is, for the most part, beyond our practical experience. That said, if we keep in mind that each of us is an essential part of ALL THAT IS, with a vast resource of knowledge encapsulated within each cell, each molecule, we keep a channel open to those resources so that what we need at any given moment is there for our use. See **Self**.

Reflection   In THE EXPERIMENT, the *reflection* is the world of appearances. Obviously, everything the eye sees is reflected light energy, but the idea of reflection goes beyond this. All the material substance that surrounds us and in fact, our entire conception of the cosmos, is considered to be a reflection of an all-encompassing energy Source, THE *Reflector*. As an analogy, think of a reflection we see in a mirror. We think of that which is reflected as the reality, and the reflection as just an image of the real thing. In THE EXPERIMENT, the medium we inhabit, the fabric of space-time, is highly reflective, like a mirror. The energy of the Source, THE *Reflector*, flows through and is shaped by, various consciousness units, ourselves included. The shaped energy is reflected by this medium to appear in any number of ways, depending upon who is perceiving it. That which we perceive we call "reality," but there are a multitude of perceivers and infinite realities, infinite reflections. As we mentioned in the Point of View, p.11-12, even two people looking into the same mirror from different angles will see completely different images, different realities.

Reflector   The all-encompassing energy Source variously known as THE ALL, ALL THAT IS, THE FORCE; the source of the *reflection*.

Self   The self is a focus point of the energy of the ALL. Again, a loosely used term that can refer to many levels of self. There is the "small me" self that is limited to the perceptions of the physical senses, or the ego. We speak of one's larger self, or oversoul as a being (ourself) with a more all-encompassing view, a guardian angel, or guide which in turn has its larger Self or teacher. Just as we raise our children to incorporate the truths that we have learned, our true Self, ALL THAT IS, guides us to become aware, at greater levels, of our essential nature.

Spoke-Focus   A term that describes the shape, or the structure, of the reality we perceive; of the consciousness that perceives it and beyond that, or within it, of the source of consciousness itself. A focus is a center of activity or awareness. A spoke radiates out from a center, but each point along each spoke is a centerpoint radiating spokes. Taken as a whole, a network of elements in constant communication with itself (see Chapter Two, The Shape of Reality, p.58-67 and Appendix C, p. 195-199).

Third eye   An organ of perception linked with the function of the pituitary gland which is said to coordinate the subconscious activities of all the systems in the body. The pituitary gland is also associated with the Ajna Chakra, between the brows, the center of telepathic communication. The use of the third eye is not encouraged in the West, and many doubt its existence, but regardless of one's position regarding this organ, the third-eye function is active in the human personality, and with persistence, practice and patience, that function can be made a part of our conscious equipment.

Three-eye view   The three-eye view incorporates the vision of the third eye to extend our perception beyond the world of three-dimensional objects. In the three-eye view, it is possible to mentally travel at an inner space level and then bring the experience back into three-dimensional space-time to enrich our earth experience.

Triangulating   When operating within the limits of three-dimensional space, triangulating is a tool for pinpointing location. When applied to perception and focus, it is a tool we can use to contact, open and integrate the third eye with the two outer eyes. This allows us to enter a meditative state and extend our awareness beyond the limits of time and space and enter into the fourth dimension. See Chapter Six, Triangulation, for more. See also, **Quadralating**.

Two-eye view   The world view that depends upon the five senses to define and interpret experience. The view that measures the boundaries of our experience in terms of tangible, visible objects.

BIBLIOGRAPHY

Carol Anthony, *A Guide to the I Ching*, Third Edition, Stow, Anthony Publishing Company, 1988.
> An excellent companion to the Wilhelm/Baynes translation of the I Ching. This book grew out of a series of meditations on the hexagrams and the situations they describe and where the Wilhelm/Baynes edition is abstract and conceptual, this guide is personal and immediate, and speaks directly to the personality engaged in the day-to-day search for clarity and guidance.

Paul Foster Case, *The Tarot, A Key to the Wisdom of the Ages*, Richmond, Macoy Publishing Company, 1947.
> For those interested in Tarot, Qabala and Hermetic wisdom, there is perhaps no finer teacher than Paul Case. This volume is an introduction to the symbolism of the Major Arcana with some beginning information on divination. The organization that he founded, the Builders of the Adytum (B.O.T.A.), in Los Angeles, offers a correspondence course on all aspects of Tarot, Alchemy, Sound and Color and Astrology.

Paul Foster Case, *The True and Invisible Rosicrucian Order*, York Beach, Samuel Weiser, Inc. 1985.
> This is a complex and fascinating work that touches on Alchemy, the Tree of Life, the Rosicrucian Grades of Adeptship and Gematria, the secret language revealed by numbers. If ever there was good reason to study Tarot, it would be to understand the deeper meanings expressed in this book.

Carlos Castaneda, *The Teachings of Don Juan, A Yaqui Way of Knowledge*, Berkeley and Los Angeles, University of Los Angeles Press, 1968.
> The don Juan teachings as related by Carlos Castaneda are a concise explanation of how we, as humans, create, perceive and relate to the world we casually refer to as reality. The first two books are centered around the hallucinatory drug experiences which, as don Juan later explained, were an attempt to dislodge Castaneda's stubborn ego from its fixation on the focus that maintains what THE EXPERIMENT has called the mirror view or the two-eye view.
>
> By the third book, *Journey to Ixtlan*, Castaneda realizes that, all along, don Juan has been teaching him to expand his perception to include the worlds, or layers of reality that extend beyond and interact with the one in which we are focused. In the fourth book, *Tales of Power*, a cliffhanger to rank with the greatest adventure stories, don Juan leads Castaneda to claim that knowledge and power. In the climactic finale to the teachings, Castaneda leaps from the edge of a precipice and dissolves his essence into the third attention.
>
> The fifth and sixth books deal with his recapitulation of the teachings and his further attempts to put them into perspective. The seventh book, *The Fire from Within*, is the crown jewel of the series, and discusses the nature

of awareness. This book is a gem. The eighth and ninth books deal with *stalking* and *dreaming* respectively.

This series has left an indelible mark upon the body of works dealing with perception and the use of awareness. Our collective consciousness has been transformed by concepts such as *impeccability, storing personal power, erasing personal history, the nagual and tonal, recapitulation*; the list goes on.

Carlos Castaneda, *A Separate Reality*, New York, Simon and Schuster, 1971.

Carlos Castaneda, *Journey to Ixtlan*, New York, Simon and Schuster, 1972.

Carlos Castaneda, *Tales of Power*, New York, Simon and Schuster, 1974.

Carlos Castaneda, *The Second Ring of Power*, Simon and Schuster, 1977.

Carlos Castaneda, *The Eagle's Gift*, New York, Simon and Schuster, 1981.

Carlos Castaneda, *The Fire from Within*, New York, Simon and Schuster, 1984.

Carlos Castaneda, *The Power of Silence, Further Lessons of don Juan*, New York, Simon and Schuster, 1987.

Carlos Castaneda, *The Art of Dreaming*, New York, HarperCollins 1993.

Robert P. Crease and Charles C. Mann, *The Second Creation, Makers of the Revolution in 20th-Century Physics*, New York, Macmillan Publishing Company, 1986.
A good description of the transition from the classical physics of the 19th Century to quantum physics and of the scientists whose work brought it about. An exciting book.

Paul Davies and John Gribbin, *The Matter Myth, Dramatic Discoveries that Challenge Our Understanding of Physical Reality*, New York, Simon and Schuster, Touchstone, 1992.
An exploration of how modern scientific discoveries have essentially rendered our common sense view of the cosmos (which, in the West, is still based on classical science) virtually obsolete.

John Gribbin, *In Search of Schrodinger's Cat, Quantum Physics and Reality*, New York, Bantam Books, 1984.
A look into the weird world of quantum physics. John Gribbin has done more to bring the mind-stretching concepts of 20th Century physics into the mainstream than any other author. Only a couple of his many books are listed here. His bibliographies are a good starting point for anyone wishing to explore this field further.

John Gribbin, *Schrodinger's Kittens and the Search for Reality*, Little, Brown and Company, 1995.
A further look at quantum physics and relativity from a vantage point of a decade later than the above work. In this book, Gribbin follows up on some of the more esoteric aspects of modern science.

Johannes Itten, *The Art of Color, The Subjective Experience and the Objective Rationale of Color*, New York, Reinhold Publishing Corp., 1961. Itten was one of the teachers at the Bauhaus and this book is based on a course in color theory that he taught there. Among other things, he covers the laws of color contrast and how they operate in our everyday perception of color.

Patanjali, *Yoga Aphorisms*, An Interpretation by William Q. Judge, Los Angeles, The Theosophy Company, 1973.
Patanjali was an ancient Indian philosopher whose aphorisms direct the student in the practice of Concentration.

The Rainbow Book, Edited by F. Lanier Graham, Revised Edition, New York, Vintage Books/Random House, 1979.
This book is a collection of the science, history, art, myth and lore concerning rainbows.

Yogi Ramacharaka, *The Science of Breath*, Chicago, The Yogi Publication Society, 1904.
This work is an invaluable aid to anyone wishing to learn the art and science of breathing. It begins with simple exercises to enhance physical vitality and moves into exercises that train the student in directing psychic or spiritual energy to heal oneself or others, to charge the personal vehicle with Prana, and finally, to make contact with one's higher soul or Self.

Jane Roberts, *Seth Speaks, The Eternal Validity of the Soul*, Notes by Robert F. Butts, Englewood Cliffs, Prentice Hall, Inc. 1972.
The Seth books, like the teachings of don Juan, stretch the reader's awareness beyond its focus on three-dimensional space-time earth perception. These books are a rich pool of concepts from which the reader may drink throughout life. Reading Seth never fails to dispel the mists (or miasms) that obscure the wondrous, limitless and humorous side of reality.

Jane Roberts, *The Nature of Personal Reality: A Seth Book*, Notes by Robert F. Butts, Englewood Cliffs, Prentice Hall, Inc., 1974.
This unique work directs the reader to discover the often hidden belief systems that determine the personal realities that we create and inhabit. Seth's advice: if you don't like your reality, look to the beliefs that form that reality and alter them to create a life that is more to your liking.

Jane Roberts, *The Unknown Reality: A Seth Book*, Volume I, Notes and Introduction by Robert F. Butts, Englewood Cliffs, Prentice Hall, Inc., 1977.
Seth's Unknown Reality is the world of probable events and life experiences, the roads not taken in our seemingly linear path through life. Each choice we make determines a life course, but at each juncture where a choice is made, many paths ray off in other directions. These paths are the probable existences that make up other aspects of ourselves and the book is directed at encouraging the reader to explore the variable selves that branch off.

Jane Roberts, *The Unknown Reality: A Seth Book, Volume II*, Notes and Introduction by Robert F. Butts, Englewood Cliffs, Prentice Hall, Inc., 1979.

Jane Roberts, *The Individual and the Nature of Mass Events, A Seth Book*, Notes by Robert F. Butts, Englewood Cliffs, Prentice Hall, Inc., 1981.
An interesting work that deals with how we collectively create and participate in mass events, from the weather to plagues and natural disasters. As with all his books, Seth emphasizes that events spring from a spontaneous dance of creativity in which our thoughts, our cells, our atoms, our dreams and those of everything around us combine at invisible (to us) levels of activity to create the world we experience.

Jane Roberts, *Dreams, Evolution and Value Fulfillment, Volume I*, Introductory Essays and notes by Robert F. Butts, New York, Prentice Hall Press, 1986.
Much of this book deals with what we think of as the origins of form. In his usual style, Seth points out the limitations of our theories of the development of life on earth. In some particularly interesting passages, he talks about how all the species existed at once (as opposed to evolving over eons), how all species experimented with creating and inhabiting form, and how the communication between the species helped each one find food, or shelter and adapt to living in a physical body.

Jane Roberts, *Dreams, Evolution and Value Fulfillment, Volume II*, Introductory Essays and Notes by Robert F. Butts, New York, Prentice Hall Press, 1986.

Charles A. Sorrell, *Minerals of the World, A Field Guide to Identification*, Illustrated by George F. Sandstrom, New York, Golden Press, 1973.
As the title suggests, a field guide, but also interesting for its discussion of the molecular substructure of the form of the mineral world, the basis of life on earth.

Michael Talbot, *The Holographic Universe*, New York, HarperCollins, 1991.
Much of this book is taken up with examples of ESP, out of body and near death experiences, miraculous events and other phenomena that remain outside the realm of orthodox scientific understanding. These stories are drawn together to support the book's central thesis which is that reality is holographic in nature. In the same way that a single holographic plate can contain numerous images, all laid down at different angles, the universe contains infinite layers of reality which can emerge from the field of probables when the perception is focused at different angles or degrees of awareness.

Three Initiates, *The Kybalion, Hermetic Philosophy*, Chicago, The Yogi Publication Society, 1912.
According to the authors of this book, the wisdom of Hermes Trismegistus, the ancient and revered Egyptian sage, is the basis of all religions and all occult systems of thought. The Kybalion is an ancient